SUBJECT ACCESS SYSTEMS
Alternatives in Design

LIBRARY AND INFORMATION SCIENCE

CONSULTING EDITORS: *Harold Borko and G. Edward Evans*
GRADUATE SCHOOL OF LIBRARY SCIENCE
UNIVERSITY OF CALIFORNIA, LOS ANGELES

Thomas H. Mott, Jr., Susan Artandi, and Leny Struminger
Introduction to PL/I Programming for Library and Information Science

Karen Sparck Jones and Martin Kay
Linguistics and Information Science

Manfred Kochen (Ed.)
Information for Action: From Knowledge to Wisdom

Harold Borko and Charles L. Bernier
Abstracting Concepts and Methods

F. W. Lancaster
Toward Paperless Information Systems

H. S. Heaps
Information Retrieval: Computational and Theoretical Aspects

Harold Borko and Charles L. Bernier
Indexing Concepts and Methods

Gerald Jahoda and Judith Schiek Braunagel
The Librarian and Reference Queries: A Systematic Approach

Charles H. Busha and Stephen P. Harter
Research Methods in Librarianship: Techniques and Interpretation

Diana M. Thomas, Ann T. Hinckley, and Elizabeth R. Eisenbach
The Effective Reference Librarian

James Cabeceiras
The Multimedia Library, Second Edition: Materials Selection and Use

G. Edward Evans
Management Techniques for Librarians, Second Edition

Irene P. Godden (Ed.)
Library Technical Services: Operations and Management

Jessica L. Milstead
Subject Access Systems: Alternatives in Design

SUBJECT ACCESS SYSTEMS

Alternatives in Design

Jessica L. Milstead

NewsBank, Inc.
New Canaan, Connecticut

1984

ACADEMIC PRESS, INC.

(Harcourt Brace Jovanovich, Publishers)

Orlando   San Diego   San Francisco   New York   London
Toronto   Montreal   Sydney   Tokyo   São Paulo

ACADEMIC PRESS, INC.
Orlando, Florida 32887

United Kingdom Edition published by
ACADEMIC PRESS, INC. (LONDON) LTD.
24/28 Oval Road, London NW1 7DX

Library of Congress Cataloging in Publication Data

Milstead, Jessica L.
   Subject access systems.

   (Library and information science)
   Bibliography: p.
   Includes index.
   1. Subject cataloging.   2. Indexing.   I. Title.
II. Series.
Z695.M673   1984   025.4   83-15721
ISBN 0-12-498120-8

PRINTED IN THE UNITED STATES OF AMERICA

84 85 86 87   9 8 7 6 5 4 3 2 1

Contents

PART III
The Collection

PART IV
Terms

PART V
Summary

Preface

During my years as designer and teacher of the design of systems for provision of subject access to documents, I often took issue with writings on this subject for their failure to consider the impact of some proposal or policy on other aspects of the functioning of indexes. It gradually became apparent to me that this was a common shortcoming. General works on system analysis show how to treat parts of systems in relation to the whole, and books on indexing consider the parts of subject access systems specifically, but no one has explicitly considered the parts of such systems in relation to their effect on the whole.

The goal of this book is to fill this gap in our understanding of subject access. Every choice—and designing any system involves a set of choices—limits other choices, and it behooves the designer to be well aware of the impact of such decisions; therefore this book is organized around the choices to be made. I begin with alternatives at the level of the file as a whole, and proceed downward to the document, the terms, and the authority for the terms. I close with influences that operate across the levels used as the basic framework.

Rather than trying to cover the entire universe of subject access, I have limited the discussion to documentary systems. The majority of such systems provide access to written rather than graphic or pictorial matter. The state of the art of provision of subject access to graphic materials is not nearly as advanced as that for written documents, and the types of material are far more variable, so that it would be extremely difficult to present the options in any coherent way.

I place no limitation on types of systems discussed in this volume; emphasis is on those that are actually working in operational situations. Systems that are still in the developmental stage are mentioned and described briefly, but they are treated as realistic alternatives only if there is some evidence of real-life use.

Developers of subject access systems and researchers in their design should find this work of value—of enough value, I hope, that they will be stimulated to take issue with it from time to time. Only thus can this volume serve to advance the state of our art.

A basic familiarity with major subject access systems and methods and how they work is assumed; the goal is to broaden such familiarity to reach an understanding of the similarities and differences in systems, and the ways in which design choices have affected their operation. Students of indexing should be able to use this work for its unique point of view as a supplement to their basic texts.

I have received invaluable assistance in preparation of this book from a number of individuals and institutions. Szilvia Szmuk and other staff members of the St. John's University Library met the challenge of my bibliographic needs so well that I was able to gain ready access to essentially all the materials I needed up to the time I left the University in 1979. It was at the Graduate School of Library and Information Science of the University of California, Los Angeles, that I first recognized the germ of the idea for this book, and much of the credit for its ever having been begun must go to the intellectual stimulation I received from my colleagues during my brief stay there. Harold Borko has generously contributed ideas, encouragement, and constructive criticism, even once curing a case of writer's block. However, the full responsibility for the final expression of the ideas of this book, together with any errors or misapprehensions, rests with me.

PART I

Introduction

CHAPTER 1

Introduction

Even though all forms of subject access are closely related, and practitioners in different parts of the field could learn a great deal from each other, issues in the area are rarely treated in general terms. Cataloguers write about cataloguing, indexers write about indexing, and classifiers write about classification, but too often they all fail to look beyond the boundaries of their own type of subject access system to see what can be learned from workers in other areas. Furthermore, the special problems of providing access by means of subjects, as distinct from other forms of access, are not usually treated as a unit. These special problems do exist, and what we know about them can be applied to all forms of subject analysis.

Because of this interrelationship, the issues are treated as a whole in this work. The common characteristics that link together subject access provision via a catalogue of books in a library, an index to journal articles, and a machine-readable database are explored. The problems of designing the file, analyzing the document, and developing criteria for index terms are quite similar, even though the similarities tend to be obscured by the artificial separation that is so prevalent. For example, for any system the designer must decide such matters as the arrangement of the file, the parts of the documents from which index terms are to be selected, and whether to use simple or complex index terms.

A subject access system may be called an index, a catalogue, a database, or even simply a guide; the essential characteristic is that it provides access to items, usually documents or parts of documents, by their subject(s). The items may be books, articles, chapters, paragraphs, illustrations, graphs, or even specific facts within the documents. This access is provided in such a manner as to avoid the necessity of scanning the entire file to reach the desired information.

It is true that most systems are limited to one, or at most a few, kinds of material, and/or to serving a limited number of purposes; the specialist working with such a system should find here guidance to exploit what has been learned by those working in different parts of the general field of subject access. Treating subject access systems as somehow different from each other just because they deal with different forms of material or different subjects, are stored in different media, or even adopt a different approach to vocabulary obscures the essential relationships among all the approaches. This work will consider those differences only as they actually affect the system design.

For instance, the fundamental difference, so far as there is one, between a list of books and one of journal articles lies not in the fact that the one is a "library catalogue" and the other a "periodical index," or even that the subject matter of works in the former is less specialized than in the latter; it is that books are significantly longer than journal articles, they are therefore on broader topics, and (ideally) each has its own apparatus to provide access to the material within it. Therefore the list of books usually need not duplicate this index apparatus. It may stop at indicating the subject(s) of the books as a whole; the periodical article list, on the other hand, will likely be the only guide to the information within the articles. In fact, one of the basic assumptions of the present inquiry—that cataloguing and indexing are the same thing—is mildly heretical even today. They both provide subject access to the contents of documents; the access provided by the tool commonly known as a catalogue may not be as thorough as that provided by the tool known as an index, but they are different in degree, not in kind. No single word has only the general connotation of provision of subject access without regard to the specific type of tool; indexing comes closest, and that word will frequently be used throughout this work to connote forms of subject access provision in general.

If they are to be educated rather than merely trained in some routines, students of any aspect of subject access (whether labeled cataloguing or indexing) need to acquire an understanding of the fundamental principles of subject analysis. This is something they cannot readily do if their study is limited to a single set of specific applications of those principles. This work approaches the exposition of those fundamental principles by showing how the choices made among alternatives interact with each other; each choice constrains a multitude of others, and it is well to be aware of these constraints.

For several decades now, the field of subject access has been in ferment. Much research has been performed and it has taught us a great deal—not as much research or as much learned from it as one could wish, but considerable results nonetheless. Conclusions have been drawn, not always fully warranted by the facts. The time has come now to see just where we do stand with the vast variety of system options available to the designer today.

This work treats the design of a system for subject access as a set of interacting choices, describing the choices together with the ways in which one choice may constrain others. Every aspect of a subject access system is the result of a choice between alternatives. Sometimes these alternatives represent an either–or dichotomy, but more often they are the extremes of a continuum, with the choice then being the optimum point on the continuum. For example, while indexes are usually considered to be either alphabetical or classified in arrangement, most contain features of both forms, even though one or the other predominates.

None of the factors is independent; each choice influences and is influenced by others. The influence may be only slight, or it may in effect predetermine another choice so that the latter is not actually a choice at all. In such a case what appears to be a choice of one option is clearly a single choice among several options, and it is well to be aware that making the single choice thus forecloses multiple options.

It is the task of the index designer to make the best possible trade-offs among these interacting options, and this is not an easy task. Our knowledge of the interactions among the options is limited, and little of it has been set down formally. Vickery (1971) has analyzed some aspects of the structure of index languages.

General research on subject access in recent years has concentrated on recall–precision studies and on costs. There has also been some—but not nearly enough—attention to development of theories of access. Added to this has been a great deal of work on design of individual systems, some of which has included development of methodologies, such as facet analysis, which are broadly applicable and have influenced all later efforts.

One thing that has been lacking in these efforts is a coordinated approach to index system design that sets down the alternatives, together with the consequences, so far as they are known, of any particular choice. The goal of this work is to fill that gap. Topics to be discussed include file design in the intellectual, not the mechanical, sense; document treatment; and the ways in which terms are generated. When applicable research is available, the effect of choices on costs or cost-effectiveness and on recall and precision are considered, but these

issues are not central to the approach of this work. Maximizing recall
and precision with the best obtainable cost-effectiveness ratios is very
important, but our knowledge of how to do this is limited, partly because in the work that has been done it has not been feasible to consider, let alone manipulate, all the factors in the system design. Worse,
our ability to develop cost–benefit ratios is practically nil. Recall and
precision are only the best-quantified, not necessarily the best, measures of retrieval quality.

More thorough studies of both retrieval and cost should become
possible as a result of the drawing together here of the options in subject access system design. The systems approach to problems, while it
has developed an entire body of literature and techniques of its own,
is basically a way of starting from a determination of the goal(s) to be
achieved (the output) and the resources available (the input) to reach a
decision on the methods to be used (the processing) to achieve the goals.
The systems approach requires study of the options and their effect on
each other. It requires that every assumption be questioned, that nothing be taken for granted. There is such a large body of unexamined
assumptions in most subject access systems today that examination of
these assumptions is a vital necessity.

Historical Background

In considering the options available for subject access system design, it is interesting to look at the historical background out of which
modern systems have grown. The treatment here is intended to help
the reader place subject access in perspective. It is not intended to be
definitive; such an effort would require a book in itself.

The oldest systems discussed in the literature would today be considered tables of contents or abstracts. That is, they are narrative or
tabular summaries of the contents of the document in more or less the
same order as the information in the document itself. Such surrogates
are intended more for scanning than for reference and are not the subject of this work.

Modern subject access systems derive from two traditions that have
grown side by side, often with little cross fertilization. These are book
indexes, which analyze the contents of a single document, and library
catalogues, which analyze the contents of a number of documents. They
derive from two different sources: the table of contents of the book,
and the inventory or shelf-list of the collection. Indexes and cata-

logues—in something approaching the modern form—arose when it occurred to someone that access to the contents of a book or collection of books would be aided by provision of a guide in a different order.

Limiting this discussion to systems that recapitulate the contents of the document or the collection in an order designed for reference and different from that of the original enables us to eliminate several millenia from consideration. It also seems to eliminate the Eastern hemisphere, since access before Western contact appears to have been limited to inventories and lists of contents. There is no evidence that Eastern scholars provided rearranged access to information before Western contact. The first known contents lists were produced by the Sumerians, but the first reference indexes date from Christian times. The first inventory of a multi-document collection goes back well into pre-Christian times, though the exact date is not certain. Daly (1967) discusses the history of alphabetization, without which many indexes as known today would of course not exist.

Witty (1973) locates the first work containing a reference aid that serves the function of a subject index in the sixth century. At this time, the *Apothegmata*, a fifth-century collection of the sayings of the Greek fathers of the Christian Church, was rearranged from its former classified order into an alphabetical one. He points out that the alphabetical index was not really practical until the codex form of the book, which lends itself to reference, was developed. The first concordance to the Bible was made by Cardinal Hugh of St. Cler in the thirteenth century (Metcalfe, 1976).

True alphabetical indexing seems to have arisen in the fourteenth century. The revival of intellectual culture in the universities of Europe and the popularity of scholastic disputation led quite naturally to a need for reference to the specific contents of books, particularly theses. These indexes consisted primarily of the keywords in the theses, or disputations, alphabetically arranged. It must be noted, however, that this arrangement was not fully alphabetical in the modern sense. The ordering extended at most through the first syllable or first three letters of the first word; frequently it did not go past the first letter. Only a few of the incunabula produced during the fifteenth century have indexes, and these were rather poorly made by present-day standards (Witty, 1973).

Meanwhile the first example of a catalogue with a subject index likewise turned up in the fifteenth century, when in 1483 a catalogue of the monastery at Melk, Austria, had three indexes—authors, subject categories, and anonymous works listed by the catchwords in their titles (Verner, 1968).

In the sixteenth century are found examples of indexes that would

be considered good today. Knight (1968) cites a 1555 edition of Polydore
Vergil's *Urbinatis Anglicae historiae*, which had a subject index, in strict
alphabetical order, with locators not merely to page but to line numbers. Part Two of Conrad Gesner's *Bibliotheca universalis*, published in
1548, is a systematic classified arrangement of the books found in the
first part of the bibliography, which was arranged by author. Also included is an alphabetical index to the subjects in the classification
scheme (Besterman, 1968). Besterman also lists other bibliographers
who provided secondary means of access to their work.

Trefleus, a Benedictine monk who published a work on library
economy in 1560, advocated five catalogues for collections, among them
a classified one (the shelf order); a subject index, presumably classified,
to the books' contents; and an alphabetical index to this subject index
(Norris, 1939). Norris offers no record of a catalogue being prepared
according to Trefleus's system.

It was in the seventeenth century that the first recorded catalogues
with subject indexes were produced and that an indexer lost his ears
for his work. The catalogue of Sion College (England), published in
1650, was a single-entry list, with anonymous works entered under
subject headings (Norris, 1939). Meanwhile, Prynne's *Histrio-mastix*
was published in 1633. According to Knight, it is said that, since the
work itself was nearly unreadable, Prynne would have been safe had
he not indexed it. *Histrio-mastix* recorded Prynne's opposition to the
stage, a particularly unfortunate subject since Charles I's queen, Hen-
rietta Maria, was rehearsing a play. A rather prolix index entry on
"whorish women" on the stage was quoted at the Star Chamber proceedings against Prynne, and he was sentenced to have his ears cut off
(Knight, 1968).

A surprisingly modern-sounding system is described by Verner
(1968). In the latter part of the seventeenth century, Adrien Baillet was
librarian and tutor to the household of Chrétien-François de Lamoignon. He prepared a catalogue of Lamoignon's library, with the main
arrangement in classified (shelf) order, and an alphabetical subject index. In the preface to his catalogue he described the system: it included
cross references, specific entry, subdivisions, and rules for choosing
among alternative words and phrases for subject headings.

While the provision of subject access to conventional forms of literature was improving, a new form, the scientific journal, had arisen
in the second half of the seventeenth century, and it was served very
poorly with retrospective access. For instance, the subject index to the
1682 volume of *Acta eruditorum* consisted of only six general categories.

By the eighteenth century, indexes were common enough to be satirized by English writers, and professional indexers began to ply their trade (Knight, 1968). It appears that, during this century and the next, the pattern for book indexes was one of gradual improvement and expansion.

It is in the area of catalogues of libraries that dramatic developments occurred during the nineteenth century. In the early years of the century the relative desirability of author versus subject-classified arrangement was at issue. Norris (1939) records a few instances of objections to the latter on the ground that a subject catalogue would show up gaps in the collection. As the century progressed, however, the issue soon became one of whether an author catalogue with a subject index was preferable to the reverse. A notable event in 1825 was Horne's proposal that books be entered in more than one place in the classed catalogue of the British Museum Library if their content warranted it. However, his work was abandoned after a few years.

By the second half of the nineteenth century, the classified catalogue was dominant in Europe, the alphabetical subject form in the United States. The earliest alphabetical subject catalogues normally used catchword entries derived from substantive words in titles. This is what Crestadoro meant by a subject index in his 1856 work, *The Art of Making Catalogues of Libraries*. Jewett included an alphabetical "topical index" in his 1853 catalogue of the Brown University Library, while Cutter's catalogue of the Boston Athenaeum Library, published in 1874–1882, established the alphabetical subject heading as the access pattern for American libraries. Cutter's (1904) rules, first published in 1876, still strongly influence library practice today. Cutter also formalized principles of the reference, or syndetic, structure.

Codification of classification schemes also began at the same time. They had grown gradually from the broad subject categories used for the presses in early libraries into highly refined hierarchical schemes based on philosophical systems of classification of knowledge. Of the significant general document classification schemes, all but Bliss and Colon began publication between 1876 and 1910.

Newspaper indexing also began in the mid-nineteenth century with the *New York Times*. Although it was indexed from its inception in 1851, the index was not published for many years, and there were gaps when no indexing was done at all. For a long time few or no other newspapers were indexed (Friedman, 1942, pp. 8–19).

It was with the development of these nineteenth century schemes that the relative locator was invented; that is, a locator that places the document or item of information, not in a fixed physical location, but relative to other items in the collection. While relative location dominates collections of separate physical documents, it has for some reason only rarely been used in indexes to books and journals.

In 1911 the Library of Congress published its subject heading list. This action imposed a kind of standardization on library catalogues in the United States, since it was cheaper for them to buy Library of Congress (LC) catalogue cards and use the preprinted headings than to do their own cataloguing.

Thus, at the beginning of the twentieth century, the following major alternatives were available to the designer of a subject access system:

1. various levels of information in the entry;
2. alphabetical or classified arrangement;
3. syndetic structure;
4. derived or assigned terms; and
5. relative or fixed location.

Postcoordination, machine search, and synthesis did not yet exist.

The beginnings of implicit facet analysis, coupled with synthetic devices on a small scale, could be seen early, for example, the Dewey Decimal Classification, or Kaiser's "concrete-process" system (Kaiser, 1911), but the inventor of the method as a consciously applied tool for indexing was Ranganathan with his "Meccano set" in the first edition of the Colon classification in 1933. His ideas have influenced all work in subject analysis since then, and it is rare today to see a new scheme without some provision for synthesis, even if the facet analysis is only implicit.

The next advances grew out of the need to control the vast bodies of information that became available after World War II. Document collections that did not look like conventional libraries—and whose administrators did not look to conventional library solutions—sprang up. The first, and most fruitful, result was the invention and popularization of postcoordinate indexing by Taube, Batten, and others. While it raised its own set of new problems, this technique solved one very vexing old one—the complex concept and how to cite it (or how much of it to cite). In a postcoordinate system the indexer breaks up the complex concept into its components for indexing; the searcher then can search on any of the parts in any order.

The 1950s brought the first use of media other than paper for storage of indexes. Indexes of document collections were keyboarded into machine-readable form for storage and search, first experimentally, but soon after operationally.

Shaw's Rapid Selector was the forerunner of microform storage devices which combined some form of indexing with the documents themselves. This branch of development has until recently found only a few highly technical applications; it has been much more common for indexes to microform collections to be stored externally, usually on paper, where they may be scanned. Recent developments promise change here, as computer and microform systems are integrated, with microform serving as the bulk storage device for the documents, and the computer maintaining the indexes.

About this time, and connected with the use of computers, there came an intellectual advance, the development of KWIC (Key Word in Context) indexing by Luhn and his colleagues at IBM. They did not invent derivative indexing; it preceded assignment indexing by centuries. What they did do was find a way to do it fast and cheaply and with no intellectual input to the individual document analysis. The first major application was *Chemical Titles,* beginning publication in 1961.

In the 1960s Cleverdon led what became a trend with his work in the Cranfield experiments on evaluation of indexing systems. These efforts have taught us a great deal about some factors in system design, but others remain elusive.

At about the same time a great deal of experimentation and research was begun into various forms of automatic document surrogation, with Salton and Sparck Jones the leading researchers. This work has suffered from a major technical limitation in that documents must exist in machine-readable form for automatic indexing to be practical; the recent integration of computers into the publishing process suggests that this obstacle may be overcome and we shall begin to see operational automatic indexing systems based on more than title and abstract information.

In the 1960s computers began to be used in the publishing industry, at first sparingly, but now fairly routinely. The use of data processing machines in the preparation of manuscripts for publication has made it possible to begin preparation of indexes at an earlier stage in the publication cycle, to update them more regularly, and to search them more conveniently. As noted above, this integration may be expected to make possible the preparation of indexes—printed, or more likely machine stored—without human intellectual intervention. One possible direction may be seen in the development of full-text databases, of which a few are presently available. In general, however, the indexing of these databases goes little beyond the simple noting of the occurrence of individual text words or phrases. While these databases have only become widely available in the past few years, it seems highly probable that the ability to search full text will affect subject analysis quite significantly.

In the late 1950s and early 1960s a greatly extended form of authority tool, the thesaurus, appeared. It grew out of the old subject heading lists, but is more carefully compiled, usually with a fully worked-out structure, in contrast to subject heading lists that have often simply grown by accretion.

In the 1960s the idea of coextensiveness was formally developed by Coates (1960) as a new solution to the problems of specific entry. For Cutter and for those he influenced, subject headings were to be specific—but the definition of specific was vague; it confused Cutter, and his followers did not do much better. Only "distinct subjects" were considered to warrant specific entry. In the classic example, Cutter stated that since the topic of "movement of fluids in plants" did not have a name, the best option available was the general heading "Botany, physiological." Miksa (1983) ascribes this apparent confusion to a way of thinking about the structures of knowledge that differs from that prevalent today. Later other authors discussed "limits" to specificity—for example, "cats," and probably "Siamese cats," but most likely not "Chocolate point Siamese cats," even for a work on that subject. With no reliable guidance available, except from past practice, solutions were at best inconsistent.

As noted above, Coates cut this knot in 1960 by proposing a new definition of specificity: the "specific" heading is the one that is coextensive, summarizing all aspects of the subject of a work. The impact of this can be seen in the PRECIS (Preserved Context Indexing System) developed by Derek Austin for the British National Bibliography.

In the mid-1970s Atherton brought together the two streams of subject analysis in an attempt to provide better access. In her Subject Access Project, she attempted to integrate the subject analysis of single documents into the index of a multi-document collection. Terms from index headings and tables of contents of books were added as enrichment to MARC (Machine Readable Cataloging) records (Gratch et al., 1978).

Wellisch (1980b) has published a comprehensive bibliography of the literature that is an essential tool for any student attempting to gain an understanding of the state of the art of indexing.

At present we have available a wide range of alternatives for subject access system design, but we lack knowledge of the ways in which they interact to influence costs or retrieval. For example, we may extract our terms from the text or assign them from an external vocabulary; while we know that this affects the way in which a search must

be performed, we do not really know whether—or under what circumstances—the total cost of the system is affected, or what is the true effect on the quality of retrieval. We may arrange a printed index in a
variety of ways; while each alternative has its fervent exponents, there
is very little evidence as to which works better, nor even an indication
of how to define what "working better" is.

At the same time it seems highly likely that in the next few years
the ways we index will change quite drastically to suit the new modes
of retrieval that are becoming available. The danger is that we may, as
has happened in the past, alter our procedures without knowing what
we are giving up.

Plan of the Work

Each chapter discusses one or a few closely related options, considering any existing research on the influence of the choice on cost
and retrieval performance. This work is divided into three parts, which
are not of equal importance: the file, the document, and the terms.

File

This part focuses on such aspects as the arrangement and structure
of the file, the mode of manipulating it, and ancillary structures to aid
users in locating the desired information. These choices essentially
govern the means of searching the file.

Document

Included in this part are the choices to be made in treatment of
individual documents, such as the source(s) of indexable matter (e.g.,
title, abstract, and text), size of indexable unit, and indexing level. The
points of view from which documents may be retrieved and the minuteness of the parts that may be retrieved will be determined by these
decisions.

Terms

This section is divided into two subsections for assigned and derived terms, reflecting the fact that most of the options for the two types
are different. Since assigned-term systems require a variety of choices
about the authority for terms, considerable attention is given to these

choices. The derived-term subsection is briefer, reflecting the more limited choices available for such systems in the present state of the art. This discussion is, however, more future-oriented than other sections, because much work that today is primarily experimental may be expected to have a more significant impact in the next few decades.

Summary of Design Options

This section attempts to integrate what has preceded by summarizing the interactions of choices made at various points in index system design. It makes few recommendations as to best choices, but may indicate the needs a particular choice will serve best.

Limitations

This book is not intended to serve as a manual on how to design an entire indexing system; several works are already available for this purpose. Rather, it treats the index itself as a problem in systems design. All aspects of the collection to be indexed are taken as given; that is, the scope and exhaustiveness of the collection itself are not considered. Determination of these and other characteristics of the broader system would require one or more other books in themselves.

Such matters as cost studies are not treated, though where comparative cost studies of the alternatives treated here exist, their findings are considered. Ideally, we would have comparative costs (including user and other intangible costs) for each of the options, with other variables held constant. If we also had available a quantification of the benefits for each option, the format of this work would be quite different, since it would then be possible to determine in each case which choice would return the most for the least expenditure. Since we do not have such cost data, and are not likely to have them in the foreseeable future, this work compares the alternatives in whatever terms are available.

Similarly, comparative studies of retrieval are far from complete. Solid information is available for certain limited situations, and these findings are incorporated here, but for the much broader territory in which studies are lacking, whatever criteria are available have been used.

PART II

The File

The Entry: Lookup Characteristics

A wide variety of kinds of information may appear in an index entry, and the designer must decide both which kinds are appropriate for a given system and how much of a particular kind should be used. This chapter takes for granted the provision of the access term and any modifications, normally the first component of the entry, and concerns itself with questions relating to the kind of information included with the term. Index terms and their structure are discussed in Part IV of this book.

Closely involved with the issue of the amount and kinds of information to appear in the entry is another question—that is, the number of stages, or lookups, required before the document is in hand. A one-stage index is not an index at all, because the document itself is filed with the term. In a two-stage index one finds with the index term information leading directly to the document. Three stages, as in KWIC indexes, where the entry leads only to a bibliographic listing that must be examined to find the information required to locate the item, are not uncommon; rarely, however, are more stages found. Obviously, a smaller number of stages requires more information to be present in the entry; hence this topic is treated in this book as part of the issue of the amount of information to be included in the entry.

The information carried with an index entry may be complete or there may be practically none at all, that is, an entry may contain a copy of the indexed item itself (a collectanea), only a single keyword and an uninformative locator such as an accession number, or any amount of information between the two extremes.

This chapter treats the following dependent variables:

1. amount of information to be provided with each entry,
2. kinds of information to be provided with each entry,

3. number of lookups required to locate the document, and
4. depending on a combination of (1) and (2) above and the size of the collection, the total size of the index.

The following independent variables limit the choices:

1. nature and size of the collection to which access is to be provided,
2. purpose of the index file, and
3. accessibility of the original items.

The primary goals are to:

1. minimize total time and effort to find answers,
2. minimize redundant content, and
3. minimize the number of lookups.

Full Text

Only very rarely is a copy of the entire document carried with each entry, primarily because of the cost in added size of the index. The larger the item of information being indexed, the less practical it is to repeat the item at every access point. Systems that adopt such a pattern may tend to limit the number of entries on the basis of physical rather than of intellectual constraints.

Balanced against these disadvantages is the advantage of a single-lookup file. Once the user locates an entry, the information is all there and there is no need to look elsewhere for the document.

Self-indexing collections are not usually considered collectanea. Dictionaries and other similar files carry all the information with each entry (though they may rely on cross references from synonyms and the like), but they are compiled as a unit. In the true collectanea, separately existing information items such as book chapters or journal or newspaper articles are indexed. In such files a copy of the document is included with each entry.

Full-text retrieval systems that have no intellectual indexing are a kind of hybrid in this categorization. Physically they are not collectanea because only a pointer to the text is stored with the index entry, but they look like collectanea to users because the text associated with the entry is retrieved essentially simultaneously with the entry itself. The physical format is the most important here because it governs the ease of access; full-text files are not treated as collectanea in this book.

Collectanea are rarely published; normally they exist in a unique copy, the most common being newspaper morgues. When small, these can be flexible, readily updated, and easy to use. Indexing is merely a matter of selecting one or more topics, clipping items, and dropping them into folders. There is an absolute minimum of extra recording. It is when the collectanea becomes larger than a personal or office file that problems arise: the indexing needs to become more complex and the sheer physical problems of manipulating and storing full text become significant.

The only major published collectanea is the Human Relations Area Files. It is published in both hard copy and microform. Hines (1961) has described this file in considerable detail, and has also performed some cost analyses to show the trade-off that might be expected if a two-stage index to the collection were provided instead of the collectanea form.

With changes in both costs and technology, Hines's specific details are out of date, but the findings remain significant. Taking a printed index produced from shingled cards as an alternative, he found that 300 copies of such an index could be produced and distributed for a little over two-thirds the cost of the existing collectanea. Including a copy of the source material to make the two tools comparable raised the cost of the index form to 105% of that of the collectanea. However, one-third of that total cost was accounted for by photocopying, a cost that has remained fairly stable while other costs have risen in the intervening years. Furthermore, computer production would reduce or eliminate many of the clerical costs of the index. Thus it seems highly probable that published collectanea are not cost-effective.

Surrogates

Kinds of Information

Locator

The only two kinds of information an index entry must contain are an index term and a locator, to identify the information being indexed and to tell where it may be found, respectively. Any other information is intended to aid users in deciding if the item is of interest. If the collection being indexed is one that exists physically, the locator usually is a physical one, showing where the information item is actually located. If the collection is a conceptual one, drawn together on some basis other than that of common physical location(s), the locator must likewise be conceptual in nature, and is frequently bibliographic for textual documents. A conceptual locator will give the information required to search another index for the location of the item in a physical collection. The locator may sometimes carry more information than simply where the document is to be found. A classification number or an author name, for example, may be part or all of the locator, and these carry substantive information content.

The choice of kind of locator is partly dictated by the physical nature of the collection and the circumstances of its gathering. It does not make much sense, for instance, to assign classification notation for the sole purpose of having it serve as a locator, but if already-assigned classes indicate physical location they might just as well be used. There is certainly no point in assigning uninformative numbers, such as accession numbers, solely to serve as locators if some other device is available; one might just as well give all information that will help in document selection decisions if other factors are more or less equal. However, if the collection exists in the form of a single document, then page or paragraph numbers of the document are likely to be used as locators. For collections that do not exist physically, such as most periodical indexes, a conceptual locator, such as the bibliographic reference, is of course the only kind that can be used.

A physical locator may be either fixed or relative; that is, it may place the item in a specific physical location, or only in relation to other items in the collection. The fixed locator may be a device such as a page number, or a shelf or drawer number. Modern classification notations such as Dewey or Colon are nearly all relative; other collections may use abstract numbers or paragraph numbers, which also place the item in relation to others. Relative location is not used nearly as often as it could be; while it is nearly universal for collections of separate printed documents and for collections of their surrogates, locators in indexes to narrative texts are nearly always fixed, even when sections less than a page in length are designated in the text by identifiers such as section or paragraph numbers that could be used as locators. Use of relative location in such works would have advantages for both user and indexer. The user would have more precise guidance to the desired information, and the index could be prepared as material became available, rather than waiting for the final form of the work. Even with the advent of computer-aided indexing systems, this advance preparation is not a small advantage, since automatic insertion of page numbers requires development and use of a lookup table. The work of Ryan and Dearing (1974) illustrates the kind of effort required for computer-aided indexing to page numbers, if indexing is attempted before these numbers are available.

The type of locator that will identify the indexed items as precisely as possible should be selected. If the index designer can influence the design of the collection itself, it may be possible to assure that information present in the collection will make searching easier. For instance, it may be possible to arrange for the use of paragraph numbers in a book. If this is the case, then indexing to these numbers will provide more precise access than indexing to page numbers. As another example, an index to a work composed primarily of short, titled items of text, such as some kinds of encyclopedias and biographical works, might refer directly to an article rather than just to a page number. If it is feasible to select a locator that can be assigned as items are indexed, rather than waiting until the end, this should be done.

Bibliographic Information

As noted above, sometimes the bibliographic information, or more generally, a description of the item, is used as a locator. The clearest instance of this type of locator is found in most periodical indexes. The information may also be supplied simply as additional description to aid the user in a decision; while this discussion is oriented toward the locator use of bibliographic information, its conclusions are generally applicable to other uses of bibliographic information in index entries. In an index to a single physical document, both bibliographic information and locator may be very brief—just a page number. However, this is not what is usually meant by bibliographic information. A bibliographic reference in the conventional sense is normally supplied somewhere in any index to a collection of separate documents. If the collection is housed somewhere near the index, it may be possible— though not necessarily desirable—to dispense with the bibliographic information, requiring the user to follow up each locator to learn which documents have been indexed.

Bibliographic information may be given in varying degrees of detail and abbreviation. The amount of detail that is essential varies with the size and nature of the collection but, especially if this information is used as a conceptual locator, it is wise to err on the side of generosity. Numerous aids are available for bibliographic references, but the most important are the *Anglo-American Cataloguing Rules* (1978) and the *American National Standard for Bibliographic References* (1977).

There has been very little research into which elements of bibliographic information are valuable, and to what extent, in helping users to decide which of the documents listed under an index term are of interest. Perhaps the most commonly reproduced item is the title of the work, followed by the author's name, with other items occurring much more rarely. The designer must make the best possible trade-off between space and information. There is a direct connection between this decision, particularly where the title is concerned, and the amount of information given in the index term or phrase.

A detailed index phrase of the sort found in the *Chemical Abstracts* indexes renders the title superfluous because it will give all the useful information from the title, together with additional information from other sources. At the other end of the spectrum is the term limited to a single word or brief phrase. In an index of any size at all, this situation cries out for more information, to save users from wading through masses of material to find relevant documents. The title is readily available, and it costs nothing in intellectual input to add it. While it can thus be less costly to include the title in the entry than to write a complex modifier, there is an offsetting set of disadvantages: one is limited to the information present in the title, which may not be particularly helpful; and the order of title words is unlikely to produce a useful subarrangement under the index term, meaning that all entries must be scanned. There seems to have been no research on whether and under what conditions it is useful to include the title in an index entry. Research comparing retrieval in searches on titles and on index terms is indirectly relevant here, but the real issue raised by that research is that of derivative and assigned indexing; the discussion of this issue may be found in Part IV.

If information intended for location purposes is abbreviated, with more extended information available via a second lookup, as in a journal list, the user may transcribe only the most readily available information, and this may not be adequate for unambiguous identification of the document. In any case, it must be remembered that if the information is provided to help in weeding out unwanted items rather than for location purposes, it is probably wise to give only that which can be understood without another lookup. To require a user to carry out a second lookup to understand information provided only to help in deciding if the item is of interest in the first place is self-defeating.

Abstract

An abstract, or narrative summary of the document, is intended to aid the user in determining whether or not the item answers a given need. Abstracts are costly to produce, store, and retrieve, though use of author-generated abstracts can cut the expense of production significantly. They are most often provided in systems that are designed for current awareness or scanning, rather than for specific lookup, though once abstracts are in a system they may be used for spin-offs regardless of initial purpose. A book-length discussion of abstracting may be found in Borko and Bernier (1975).

Abstracts may vary in length from brief annotations to several hundred or even a thousand words. Their length is a function of both system design and the individual document. While they are normally in a narrative format, a telegraphic style or even a list of key phrases may be used to serve the purpose of summarizing the documents. Hirayama (1964) seems to have carried out the only study of length of abstracts. Five abstracts of different lengths, none written specifically for this investigation, were compared. The number of "facts" in the original article and in each abstract was computed as a function of length. While longer abstracts did contain more facts, shorter abstracts were found to be more efficient, in that the ratio of facts to words was higher. Hirayama did not report any attempt to determine if shorter abstracts were more tightly written. It seems possible that the tighter the requirements in terms of length limitations, the more likely the abstract writer is to write tersely, getting more facts into a given wordage. If this were the case, then application of similar standards could make longer abstracts just as efficient.

Other Information

The other kinds of information about index items that may be included in entries are limitless, and coverage here will be limited to examples. Illustrations or the lack of them may be specified, as may be the language of the documents and/or of a summary. Size, shape, running time, operating equipment and other factors that may affect usability are candidates for inclusion. Intellectual level or viewpoint may be coded, either as part of the index heading itself, or in the body of the entry. Other index terms assigned to the document may be listed as a means of better indicating the subject. The advent of machine retrieval systems has made coding of extra information appear more desirable, as it can be used directly in a search. In a human-searched system, access points are rarely provided for such information; if it is in the entry at all the user must scan for it. No item of information should be provided just because it is available; adding it to the record, sorting it, and retrieving it are all costly. The needs for and uses of the index should be carefully considered in the design, with only the information that can be of value supplied.

Deciding How Much Information to Include

The decision as to how much of the possible information to include with each entry is a complex one, determined by a number of factors.

Levels of Information

Different levels of information may be used in the file, in either separate subfiles or integrated ones. For instance, an abstract is very rarely given more than once in a file, because it takes up so much space. There may be a separate subfile of abstracts with index references as in most abstracting and indexing services, or they may be integrated with the main file, references being provided from other access points to the one containing the abstract, as in the *New York Times Index* or in parts of *Library Literature* from 1933 to 1957.

When bibliographic and other data are very complex or lengthy, they may also be provided in different degrees of fullness at different access points, whether in separate or integrated subfiles. Different forms of material or levels of subject may likewise be treated with different levels of completeness, according to editorial policy.

If the entry with brief information refers the user to another entry with more thorough information, whether integrated or separate, one has in effect imposed an extra lookup on the users, from index to main file to document itself. Sometimes system considerations make such a choice inevitable, as when providing enough bibliographic information to permit the user to skip the main file would increase the size of the index by two or more times. This is often the case in an abstracting and indexing service, where providing enough bibliographic information in the index entries to avoid the necessity for the user to refer back to the abstract unless she or he wanted to could well mean that the total number of index entries would have to be reduced to keep the index size manageable. In other situations, however, for instance in many book or microform library catalogs, a locator that leads directly to the document can be used; this locator may either serve as the locator for the full entry, or may simply be an additional one.

It is highly desirable, within other system constraints, to minimize the number of lookups required of the user to go from index access to document.

Number of Entries in the Index

While there is a perfectly normal temptation to cut the amount of information given with each entry in order to save space as the index grows larger, just exactly the opposite policy is necessary. An important criterion of good indexing is that the user need not sort through many undifferentiated entries to locate those that are useful. Therefore, the longer the index, or more importantly, the more entries per main heading, the more vital it is to provide help in selecting items. This may be done by means of subdivisions or modifications of the index heading itself (as treated in Chapter 9) or by provision of greater detail about the document.

Storage Requirements

The larger the number of entries in an index, the more vital it becomes that each item of information provide a payoff for the space it consumes. This produces a direct conflict with the aforementioned need to add more information as the number of entries increases. A trade-off becomes necessary between user effort and system costs. Regrettably, users tend to come off second best, largely because the system design frequently does not take them fully into account, and even if it tries to do so, user effort is extremely difficult to quantify. It is easy to demonstrate the cost of providing an extra line of information in the index; it is possible, though it is rarely done, to quantify the time cost to the user of going elsewhere to look for that information; but it is next to impossible to ascertain the cost of the frustration and missed information because the user perceives the extra trouble as not worthwhile.

Accessibility of the Original Item

Since the whole purpose of providing index access in the first place is to decrease the effort required of the information seeker, an important factor in the decision on how much information to provide with each index entry is the accessibility of the original information item. The entry cannot enable one to predict with 100% certainty which items will serve a given need; the object is to reduce to a minimum the number of useless (for a given query) items that must be examined while maximizing the useful retrieval, and the reason for minimizing useless retrieval is to save user time and effort. Therefore, if locating the information item is merely a matter of turning a few pages and perhaps scanning a few lines (several columns of fine print is another matter), the user effort is far less than if, to take the opposite extreme, the item is stored in microform at a distant location, there is a charge to get it, and it is in a language not read by the user. In the former instance, the user will not find it very troublesome to examine a few items to determine if they fulfill the need; in the latter, the user is unlikely even to try to retrieve the document, let alone have it translated, unless the entry has given enough information to show quite clearly that the item is almost certainly very valuable. Many cases fall between these extremes, of course, and in general the accessibility of the original should be a strong governing influence on the amount of information provided with each entry.

Purposes of the File

A file intended for current awareness scanning should provide more information than one designed solely for reference lookup, while the kinds of information required for a file intended for specific fact location are entirely different.

For scanning, the material should be arranged in categories, few enough, and with enough entries in each, so that the user will find most or all of the items of interest near each other. There should also be enough information to permit reasonable certainty about the value of the document, that is, an abstract is desirable. For reference lookup it is useful to be able to go to a specific term, and while abstracts are helpful, they are not quite as vital if the index terms are precise enough to do their job. For specific fact search, the entry must of course indicate and provide access for the specific fact in question.

Research Studies

If original, abstracts are very costly to write; whether original or author prepared, they add significantly to the bulk of a system. Therefore, it is of interest to learn whether or not they are worth the cost of inclusion. There is a good deal of research bearing indirectly on this issue, in the form of studies comparing title- and abstract-based indexing. (Including an abstract, but not a title, seems never to have been seriously considered for systems in which the documents have true titles.) Saracevic (1969) studied this issue from the point of view of prediction of relevance, finding that 83% of judgments from titles were confirmed by the full text, while full text confirmed 90% of judgments based on abstracts. However, his findings regarding recognition of relevant documents are considerably less favorable: 63% from titles and 77% from abstracts. Abbot, Hunter, and Simkins (1968) found that the relevance of a fairly high proportion of the documents produced as a result of SDI (Selective Dissemination of Information) searches of chemistry data bases could not be judged from titles alone. The range, by profile, was from 0 to 57%. Thompson (1973), however, in reviewing the literature of relevance judgments, concluded that abstracts do not affect the relevance decision very much.

In studies comparing indexing or searching on the basis of titles and abstracts, the results are different. Maloney (1974) found that, of items located by means of text searching both title and abstract, only 27% would have been located by searching on the title alone.

Thus, it is not easy to determine if inclusion of abstracts is warranted. Probably the need is strongly situation dependent, including such factors as the informativeness of titles in the universe indexed, the kinds of needs the users are experiencing, and the minuteness in detail of the indexing. Since the concern here is not with retrieval on the basis of abstracts (this is in the domain of free text search, treated in Part IV), but rather with having them present for examination, the relevance judgment findings probably should receive more weight.

Another factor, which seems never to have been studied in these terms, is the accessibility of the original documents. If the originals are conveniently accessible, it is more reasonable to force the user to go directly to them from the index entry than if they are remotely located.

Levine (1974) found that when an automated fiche retrieval device was made available, users tended to make their searches simpler and broader, apparently because they could so conveniently move to the entire document. While this account is not based on a study made under controlled conditions, it is thought-provoking and seems to confirm that accessibility of the original does play a part in the design of indexes.

Future Trends

The growing potential of full text storage means that in the foreseeable future it may be possible in some situations to design a system that appears to provide one-step access, in which the user poses a query and in return receives immediate access to documents that provide the answer. Today there are a number of systems providing such direct access to abstracts only; the lack of machine-readable full text and the cost of storing it online are the factors that compel this limitation. True, such online access is not really direct; a separate index is computer-searched for document numbers (locators) and the abstracts are only retrieved as a result of a second request. The important thing is that to the user at the terminal, the system looks as if it is providing direct access. The intermediate step appears to the user as an opportunity to consider whether the amount of retrieval meets the need or not.

There are a few systems that do provide such access to the full text of documents. These are clearly going to become more important in the future, but storage of full text will remain relatively costly, limiting such files to areas in which the costs can be justified. The ideal, of course, since many texts are discursive and/or give a great deal of space to background information that may not be of great interest for retrieval purposes, will be a system that provides full-text access to extracts of those portions of documents containing information that will be useful for retrieval.

For printed indexes, however, and for the next few years in most machine systems, it will be necessary to make do with less than full text with every index entry. Therefore the problem is to decide how much information to provide.

Summary

Indexes, known as collectanea, which provide copies of full text with each entry, exist primarily in unique copies, and it seems not to be cost-effective to publish them. Even in a single copy they become unwieldy as soon as they grow beyond a very small size, tending to limit the amount of material included in them. Full-text databases may appear as collectanea to users, but they are not physically stored as collectanea, and since they have few of the distinguishing limitations of collectanea, they are not treated as such in this work.

Aside from the index term information itself (index terms are discussed in Part IV), there are three major candidates for inclusion in the index entry: locator (required), bibliographic information, and abstract. The purpose of the optional information is to aid in the decision as to whether a reference is worth pursuing. While the locator must be present, it may vary greatly in detail. Bibliographic information may be provided, as may an abstract. The major factors in the decision on the amount of information to provide are the number of entries under index terms, balanced against increases in costs due to size; accessibility of the original; and the purpose for which the file is intended to be used. Different levels of information may be provided in different parts of the index, causing it in effect to serve as an index to itself for some searches. What research there has been has concentrated on the relative value of titles and abstracts. While the results are conflicting, there seems to be some evidence that abstracts do aid in the relevance decision. There has, however, been no attempt to quantify the value against the cost of including the abstract.

CHAPTER 3

Modes of Storage and Search

Introduction

Until about 50 years ago, there would have been little need for a chapter on this topic. For practical purposes the only way to store an index was in the form of entries on paper or an equivalent medium; such an index could only be searched by the unaided human eye. The available choices were between card and page form, and there were only a few very limited options in updating. Furthermore, the only file organization for such a system was the item-on-term mode typified by card catalogues, in which a separate entry or reference is made for each subject or point of view to which access is desired. In this mode the index term is the access point, and attached to each term is a list of all the documents indexed by that term.

All this began to change in the early 1950s. Certain basic concepts and techniques had been developed before then, but their practical influence on indexes was minimal. A patent covering the use of correlative principles in the form of punched cards for bird identification was issued around the turn of the century, but there is no record that it influenced later developments. The first applications of microfilm were to whole documents, with indexes remaining in hard copy form.

In the early 1950s Mortimer Taube and others began the development of postcoordinate indexing. With this technique the posting of a term to an item became a realistic alternative. With term-on-item procedures the index is a set of document records, each containing a list of all the index terms posted to that document, rather than a set of term records, each containing a list of all the documents posted to a term. Most systems using edge-notched cards are of the term-on-item type.

The entry on the card describes the document, and the punches around the edge of the card are codes for all the index terms assigned to the document.

Hand in hand, though usually in item-on-term form, came the use of punched card systems, where the information is stored in a form (holes in specified positions) that must be converted before the human eye can conveniently read it. Either form may be used in postcoordinate systems.

Since that time the range of options has increased dramatically. Indexes may be stored in eye-readable copy or microform; in media that operate on the basis of coincidence of holes at specific coordinates, or in computer-readable media, today normally magnetic, but in the future probably including a wide diversity of materials.

This chapter is concerned primarily with what might be called physical modes of storage and search: the medium and the file organization. Other chapters deal with the intellectual modes of storage and search. While the physical modes are certainly of more importance than this allocation of space would imply, this book is not really concerned with physical file organization and search except as they directly influence intellectual organization, and the treatment in this chapter reflects that limitation.

The variables treated are:

1. the entity (human or machine) performing the search,
2. whether the search is performed in real time,
3. term manipulation method,
4. file organization,
5. number of files, and
6. storage medium.

The goals are to:

1. maximize search speed,
2. minimize subject analysis costs, and
3. keep file size manageable.

Modes of Search

Search methods may be categorized on the basis of the entity doing the searching (human or computer) or on the basis of the method of manipulation of terms (pre- or postcoordinate).

Human versus Computer Search

Search methods fall into two basic categories: human and computer; search of card-form postcoordinate systems may be treated as a variant of human searching. Most of the advantages and disadvantages of each are those of their respective storage media, but there are other factors to be considered. Human lookup can exploit the immense serendipitous and browsing capabilities of the human mind, which can recognize what it is looking for even if the goal is only vaguely specified in advance. At the same time, however, the human is fatigue prone, and must undertake a separate operation in order to record the findings of a search.

A computer search is, of course, human-directed at some stage, but the computer does the actual examination of the index. A computer searches very fast, is not fatigue prone, and can readily make a copy of the retrieved information as it goes along; but it is very literal minded, and a slight error in instructions can ruin a search entirely or seriously diminish its value. Computer search is likely to appear more expensive than manual search, but this is largely because the cost of the user's time in searching is often not included in the cost accounting. Studies that include user time as a factor usually find that computer search is cheaper (Elchesen, 1978).

If an index is to be searched both by humans and by computers, as is the case with more and more indexes today, very careful design is required to maximize the effectiveness of both means of searching. Most existing indexes are designed primarily for one or the other mode, and searching via the secondary mode is likely to be either difficult, not very effective, or both. For example, many new indexes designed in the past 15 years to produce both a printed product and a computer-searchable data base use thesauri of terms that are relatively simple in structure, relying on postcoordination of several terms to produce a complex query for machine search. This is all well and good, but if the printed index uses the same simple terms, far too many documents for effective search will accumulate under some terms, and the usual printed index has no devices to make postcoordination more convenient. The end result can be long lists of unusable entries, requiring paper and ink to print and bind and shelf space to store, while effectively depriving the user of important access points to information.

Economics has a great deal to do with the choice between human and computer search. If the system cannot support computer access, then human search is the only alternative. Assuming that both options are economically viable, however, the kinds of questions that are expected to be addressed to the file are a major determinant of the choice. If the file is a relatively simple one and simple questions are expected, computer search may not be worth the cost. On the other hand, if searches are to be complex, with many facets varying from search to search, or if the index requires updating, computer search will be preferable.

For complex searches in a manual system it is essentially impossible to provide all the access points that will be required; one is almost forced to use a lesser number of precoordinated terms. In a computer system, however, using a large number of simple terms that then may be coordinated at search is easily managed.

Unless an index is maintained on cards or some other updatable medium, forcing it to remain essentially unique, the economics of reprinting the same entries over and over again make it impractical to maintain the index in a single file; it is necessary to cut it off and start a new file at fairly frequent intervals. If the file is not to be updated, or if queries are strongly time related, this is not a major consideration, but for the majority of sizable indexes it is significant.

Batch versus Online Search

This pair of search modes is normally and most usefully treated as two types of computer search, but another conceptual distinction may be made that shows this typology to be a distinction applicable to human search also. Online search may be regarded as the computer form of a search performed at the time of need, either by or with direct input from the end user, and with the capability of feedback. In this context, batch or offline search is delegated, performed on the searcher's rather than the user's schedule, and therefore permits only minimal feedback. Similar characteristics may be present in human searches. This conceptualization should not be carried too far, but it aids in seeing that important features such as immediacy in feedback in online search and efficiency for massive searches in batch search have their counterparts in human searching.

Usually online search is more expensive in computer time, but less costly in user time; the ease of revising the search while it is underway or immediately after completion makes it possible to test queries and refine them on the basis of interim results. Once the kind of results a question will produce is known, that question may then be searched in batch mode on a continuing basis or against a larger (e.g., retrospective) file at far less expenditure of resources than with repetitive or massive online searching.

Term Manipulation

Coordination of Terms

The concept of postcoordination of terms is about the only one that may be regarded as truly "new" in the development of indexing in the past half century. A postcoordinate system is set up so that at the time of search the user may conveniently determine which items have been indexed by the same two or more terms, thus providing a great deal more flexibility in both indexing and search. This flexibility is not without penalty, as will be shown later in this chapter.

Mortimer Taube is generally considered to be the inventor of co-ordinate indexing (now better referred to as postcoordinate indexing, to distinguish it from conventional, or precoordinate indexing). He was soon followed by others who developed and expanded on the concept; the whole field of computer-based indexing and searching in its present form would literally be inconceivable without it.

A variety of media and formats may be used for postcoordination; they are cited here only to give some idea of the range of possibilities. Term cards usually provide spaces to write in the numbers of documents identified by a given term while item cards (rarer) have space allocated for each term. Various printed formats make it possible to put postcoordinate indexes in hard copy form, but the method that is becoming dominant today is computer search. The influence of these media on indexing choices is covered in the final chapter of this work.

As originally conceived by Taube, postcoordinate indexing had two major advantages: (1) indexing in his Uniterm system was essentially a clerical operation involving underlining of words in text; and (2) postcoordination permitted each term to appear in the index only once and always as an access point, while at the time of search the user could make any desired combination, even those that could not have been anticipated at the time of indexing. Except as less complex terms may be used in postcoordinate indexing, the first point is one of derivative, not of postcoordinate, indexing, and it will not be further considered here.

Postcoordinate indexing does have the advantages noted. Terms may be simpler since it is assumed that the user will build in the detail required to sort out more nonrelevant documents at the time of search. Every term is an access point, and there is no problem of deciding the citation order within complex terms. Postcoordinate indexing is made to order for machine search with the computer's ability to apply elementary rules of logic faultlessly.

On the other hand, some words are meaningless, or have different meanings, in isolation; they take their significance from the word(s) with which they co-occur. It is pointless to separate the words solely to force the user to put them back together again. Postcoordination in a printed index ranges from cumbersome to impossible, depending on the format. Worst of all, the fact that two terms have been used in indexing a document does not mean that they were actually used in relation to each other; if they were not, irrelevant documents may be retrieved.

The above discussion is purposely simplified to present the problems of the "pure" format of pre- and postcoordinate indexing. However, very few precoordinate systems are "pure" in the sense that they always present the entire subject of the item in one precoordinated term. Commonly, a very complex concept that does not occur in the system with great frequency will be broken down into two or more constituent concepts and separate entries made for each. However, in the sense that no provision short of the ability to note which items are indexed in both places is made for coordination at the time of search, the system remains purely precoordinate for all practical purposes.

It is in postcoordinate systems that hybridization is fundamental. In the first place, some words (e.g., urinalysis) as Lancaster notes (1972, pp. 6-7) are precoordinated in themselves; he points out that to split these and others that are less obvious compounds (a thermometer is an instrument for measuring temperature) requires semantic factoring. Semantic factoring procedures, though developed at Case Western Reserve University, seem never to have been applied in practice and will not be considered here.

Even at the whole-word level, however, Taube himself soon introduced the concept of "bound" or precoordinated terms. Rules for deciding when to precoordinate are varied but they essentially boil down to two criteria: (1) when the meaning of the phrase is not the simple Boolean intersection of the separate words or (2) when the phrase occurs so often that to break it apart would cause an undue amount of work in retrieval.

An example that fits both criteria is "birth control." This phrase does not refer to "control of birth," and it occurs as a phrase so regularly that it is not useful to separate the components, the more so since documents on "birth control" will not be of interest to a searcher interested in either "birth" or "control."

Links and Roles

These are a pair of refinements of postcoordinate indexing that were introduced very early as devices to minimize false retrievals. Links show that two terms are actually treated in relation to each other in a document, rather than merely appearing together fortuitously, while roles show the special meaning or facet of a term that is used. Taube (1961) early described the respective uses of the two devices. The intent of links is to divide up a document into two or more parts, while roles show relations. In his example, "lead coatings for copper pipes" requires the use of roles, not links, to prevent retrieval in a search for "copper coatings" or "lead pipes," while permitting retrieval in a search for "coatings for pipes."

A number of studies (e.g., Lancaster, 1968; Landau, 1969) indicate that use of links and roles may improve precision of retrieval slightly, but at the cost of a drop in recall and at a really significant increase in cost of indexing and storage. They have also been found difficult to apply consistently. While some systems developed with roles and links continue to use them, few new systems being developed today seem to apply them at all. A major exception is PRECIS, for which use of roles is a fundamental part of the system. Artandi and Hines (1963) showed that roles and links serve essentially the same purposes as modifiers in conventional indexing practice.

Thus the designer must first choose between pre- and postcoordinate indexing; then if the latter is chosen, further decisions are required as to the degree of precoordination to be used and whether or not to apply roles and links. Furthermore, postcoordinate indexes are often searched in a precoordinate mode, that is, on the individual terms without the benefit of Boolean logic. This happens when an indexing system is available in both machine-readable form, with a vocabulary designed for machine search, and as a conventional printed index. Note that there are unconventional forms of hard copy that do permit coordination at output, however.

Weighting

Particularly in full-text retrieval systems some device is frequently needed to indicate the relative significance of an indexing term. While manual applications exist, systems going beyond two levels of weighting (e.g., print and machine-search-only terms) are very rare today. More important is the research underway on weighting in full-text systems. The weighting is practically always on the basis of some form of frequency of occurrence, be it raw frequency, frequency relative to frequency in natural language or in the collection, or some other criterion. Frequency of single words and/or of phrases may also be calculated. Sparck Jones (1974) describes the options available. On retrieval a minimum weight is set for each term or set of terms on the basis of their importance to the query. Most such systems are still experimental; relatively little application has been made to date in operational full-text systems, presumably because of the extra sophistication required by weighting procedures. Bookstein (1980) offers a theoretical procedure for using weights in conjunction with Boolean logic—an approach that may find practical application in the future.

Choosing a Method of Term Manipulation

An index that is to exist only in published printed form is generally best produced in a precoordinate format. Except for such indexes as those in the backs of books, these are becoming a rarity today, and a back-of-the-book index, being closed and therefore predictable, can repeat entries under different expressions of the same concept if needed, thereby fulfilling to at least some extent the same needs as those served by the postcoordinate form. If an index is to be machine-searchable, at this time it makes sense to provide for a reasonable amount of postcoordination of terms, though not for use of roles and links. There is no point in breaking apart words that will only be sought as phrases or which have meaning in a phrase distinct from the meanings of the individual words, and weighting procedures are still not thoroughly tested in operational systems.

Furthermore, if the index will be used both with and without postcoordination, it must be designed to be searchable in both modes. The precoordinate mode has traditionally been skimped in these situations; relatively simple terms, each attracting a large number of entries, have been used, on the assumption that retrieval would be narrowed by means of Boolean logic. When this facility is unavailable, however, the searcher has to choose between wading through a large number of entries and simply giving up.

Yet it is perfectly possible to provide for both means of search by judicious use of subheads and modifiers in the printed index; these can then be treated as separate terms for machine search, permitting the index to serve adequately in both modes.

File Organization

Physical organization in computer-stored files, while extremely important, is not the focus of this discussion. The concern here is with the impact of physical organization of files, whether computer held or not, on their intellectual organization. In all kinds of systems a choice must be made between direct and inverted organization, while in a machine system designed for online search, the kinds of indexes provided become a more important issue. Furthermore, the decision of whether to organize the index into single or multiple files also constrains other decisions.

Direct Versus Inverted Organization

In a direct file the document is the unit around which the file is organized, and the record of a document contains the full record of its subject analysis, while in an inverted file the subject term is the unit of organization, with information about each document indexed by a given term attached to the term. The former is also known as "term on item," and the latter as "item on term," to indicate which, index term or indexed item, is the basic organizational element to which the other is posted. The file organization of nearly all printed indexes is inverted; some also have a direct file, but only rarely (as in the ERIC system's *Resources in Education*) does this file actually contain all the information associated with the document. Far more typical is the bibliographic citation and abstract, with index terms omitted.

The choice between direct and inverted storage of a machine file depends on the search use to be made of it. For batched searches, direct organization is usually more efficient, but some form of inverted organization is presently essential if online search is planned.

Inverted organization imposes significant overhead in storage costs, because a record is generated for each required access point, rather than a single record for the document. The greater the number of access points per document, the greater this overhead. The trade-off between storage costs and access needs, more than any other single factor, tends to limit the size of printed indexes.

A complicating factor in the trade-off is the amount of information carried with the entry, as discussed in Chapter 2. Briefly, storage cost is based essentially on the size of the file; more entries can be fitted into a given space if the information supplied with each is reduced. However, users depend on the information in the entry for aid in deciding if the item is of value to them, so the trick is to determine which information elements are of most value in this decision.

In machine-held files the equation is similar but not identical. On the one hand, access to the full record from the inverted entry can be automatic, so that the user does not have to be aware that the entire record is not stored at the point of access. Therefore, only the information required to locate the record need be stored at each access point. On the other hand, due to the requirements of physical file organization, ten 10-character machine records usually require more space than one 100-character record.

A combination of inverted and serial search can add to the flexibility of computer search while lessening storage overhead. Indexes permitting independent search on certain elements, such as date, language, or document type, may not be generated, letting the system provide for examination of the records retrieved via index search to select the ones that meet other criteria such as those above. The trade-off here becomes quite complex, and any system designer intending to use such a capability must be careful to minimize the length of the expected serial search. The techniques for doing so are beyond the scope of this book; they may be found in works on computer file organization.

Computer systems specifically designed for associative search have recently become commercially available. At present they would be cost justifiable only for very large applications, but if their use spreads there may be a change in the relative advantages of direct and inverted file organization.

Indexes to Machine Files

The factors in deciding the number and types of access points are conceptually similar to those for conventional media, but the capabilities of computer search and the economics of computer access change the scale of the decision quite drastically. It has thus become common to provide access via not just the usual index terms, but by such items as all significant words in certain fields or even in the entire record. We are still learning how best to exploit such capabilities, because simply having more words on which to retrieve does not automatically improve access.

As noted above, access may also be available on a variety of non-subject terms, such as physical characteristics of the documents.

Number of Files

Multiple Indexes

The standard practice (American National Standards Institute, 1974) is to prepare only one index, arranging all entries of whatever type in a single file. However, it is quite common for indexes to be divided into several files on the basis of the type of entry.

It is desirable to have only one file in order to avoid confusion for users, who may not have in their minds a clear distinction among various entry types. Furthermore, users are likely not to read introductory material or to pay attention to other aids that may be provided.

On the other hand, the differences between certain kinds of headings, such as authors and chemical compound names, may be so great that interfiling them is likely to be confusing; or there may be such a disparity among the number of entries for two or more types that it seems desirable to segregate the smaller grouping into its own file.

Sometimes the sheer size and complexity of the file seem to dictate some form of separation, as in many library catalogues. It is essential to make sure that the end result in such a case is not even more confusing, as often happens with these same library files. It seems that unless a strict division by type of entry (e.g., author, title, subject) is used, even the developers of the file find it difficult to decide what should go where. Of course, it has been shown that users do not clearly distinguish between subjects and titles in catalogues (given library practice in using them as substitutes for each other this is not surprising) so even this kind of arbitrary division is likely to be confusing for the users of the file.

If the principle of division of the file is such that no duplication of entries is required, multiple indexes are likely to be less costly to produce than a single file, since the difficulty of inserting entries causes the cost of maintenance to increase more than linearly with the size. It is possible to avoid certain complex and time-consuming decisions on arrangement, for example, by simply dividing the file so that decisions as to relative location do not arise.

Cumulation

Technically this is a special case of the multiple indexes issue, but it presents enough unique problems to warrant separate treatment. Assuming the collection to be indexed is one that is supplemented from time to time, it is necessary to determine whether to update the index itself or to add new, unintegrated files at intervals. If the single file is not updated indefinitely, it in effect becomes a group of files segregated on the basis of date of addition of items to the collection.

It is effectively impossible to cumulate a single file forever. Sooner or later, whatever the method of storage, it will become impractical to continue to add entries and too cumbersome to search them. Furthermore, few information needs really require access to literally everything regardless of date. At the same time, depending on the frequency of updating the file of information, it is usually highly desirable to provide some cumulation, rather than providing a separate index to each update.

The question therefore becomes not whether to cumulate but at which intervals to do so. The storage medium is the ultimate determinant here. If the index is printed on paper, all the entries must be repetitively reprinted with each cumulation, a very expensive procedure. If maintained on cards, the file may be updated as needed for a very long time; while if it is computer-stored, the search time eventually becomes a limiting factor.

Storage Media

Only the device or medium that users must exploit to gain access to the information is of concern here. For example, an index, the machine-readable form of which exists solely to ease the preparation of its printed form, will be examined from the point of view of the printed index, not of the computer-stored version.

This course of procedure has been adopted because the mode of storage for housekeeping purposes is no longer really a matter of issue. If an index is to be updated, cumulated, or in any other way modified, only computer storage permits such operations to be performed in an economical and timely fashion. Even where these manipulations are not envisioned, only lack of facilities or knowledge limits computer usage today.

There are three major—computer-readable, print, and microform—and a number of minor storage media.

Print

Print, or hard copy, is unique among the available storage media in that it can be read directly without the interposition of any other device except, for some people, eyeglasses. Set against this truly enormous advantage are a number of disadvantages. The print form is bulky and expensive to produce; if it is maintained as a list the index must be reproduced in its entirety in order to revise it. If maintained as unit records (e.g., a card file) it is extremely costly to reproduce and is highly susceptible to damage by the unrecognized loss of records.

Microform

While there are a number of microform indexes, they are quite rare by comparison with printed and computer-readable indexes. An index in microform is essentially the same as a printed index, but greatly reduced in size—and requiring a reading device for use. A large index can be produced and updated more economically in microform than in print, especially if computer output microform is used. As a result, the use of microforms for such products as library catalogues, which require frequent updating, is on the increase. However, indexes that should be usable without artificial aids must remain in the print medium.

Computer-Readable

This category embraces all forms that must be processed by computer to be usable by humans. As noted above, situations in which the computer-readable form is solely a predecessor to print or microform are not under consideration here. Furthermore, the relative advantages of different computer-readable media are treated thoroughly in the literature, so these will also not be covered. The purpose of this section is to compare computer-readable media with other media, not with each other.

To search these media requires a computer, a very expensive machine even in its smaller versions. However, the use of this machine confers enormous benefits in economy and speed of search. It is far easier to change one's mind with a computer-readable file. If the data item is present in identifiable form, it can be made retrievable, even if it was not originally intended to be, by redesigning the system rather than by re-indexing all the records. While making data elements identifiable imposes costs in time, the cost in storage is minimal. (Making these elements searchable can be a different matter, but still is likely to demand far fewer resources than the equivalent in another medium.)

This may be illustrated quite dramatically by the example of the words of a text. Before computers the only such indexes were concordances, each usually representing a lifetime of effort, to a few of the greatest literary works. When it became possible to use the computer to sort and print bibliographic data, KWIC indexes and their variants appeared, providing access to the words in titles. When direct computer search, without the intervention of the printed medium, became available, access to the words in abstracts spread quickly and today full texts of some kinds of works are widely available for search.

Similarly, it becomes feasible to provide access on the basis of co-occurrence of terms, without having to make a decision, or requiring the user to anticipate, which of two or more terms should receive priority. Since the number of possible permutations of a multiterm concept increases as the factorial of one less than the number of terms being permuted, it is never possible to provide this kind of access for more than two or three terms at a time in a printed or microform index, but it is fairly routine in computer searching.

Minor Media

Coincidence card systems are the most important of the minor media. While they are conceptually the same as a printed index containing only index terms with accession numbers, and some contain exactly this physical information, their format makes them different in use. Whether edge-notched, optical coincidence, or with lists of accession numbers, such systems rely on matching of coordinates, usually numbers or holes. The presence of the same number, or of holes in the same positions, on the cards for two different terms, indicates a document indexed by those two terms.

Such systems, if inverted (item on term), are limited to the number of documents that can be recorded on one card; if direct (term on item) they are limited to the number of terms that can be recorded on the card. Additional sets of cards or various codings can be used, but all of these add to the overhead of what is essentially a type of system suitable primarily for relatively small applications. Furthermore, the index usually exists in one copy or at most a few copies; if there is more than one, each copy must be updated individually.

A hybrid form is the dual dictionary. With this mode, index terms are printed with their accession numbers in book form. The user receives two copies of the index, so that the lists of document numbers under two different terms can be compared side by side. Of course, with the introduction of the page format a larger number of documents can be accommodated, but there is a compensating disadvantage in that long columns of numbers must be scanned, and coordination of more than two terms requires preparation of interim lists.

Summary

Most aspects of the relationships among the features of systems covered in this chapter are fairly obvious and do not require extensive discussion. For computer search to be undertaken the information obviously must be computer stored, while it must be stored in human-usable format for human search. Complex searches covering a long period of time are best carried out by computer; if the need is only vaguely formulated, it will be useful to take advantage of the serendipitous effects of human search at least part of the time.

If both human and computer search are to be carried out, the file must be carefully designed for both modes to be effective.

Precoordinate search is usually preferable for human lookup on printed pages, while postcoordination makes better use of computer capabilities. However, almost all postcoordinate files are precoordinated to the extent of not dividing terms that are best searched as a unit; the criteria for the extent of precoordination must be individually determined for each situation.

With present technology any kind of immediacy in searching requires some form of inverted file organization. Associative systems exist but their cost is still prohibitive. Inverted organization imposes significant storage overheads, and for batched computer searches a direct file organization, requiring serial search, is satisfactory.

It is usually preferable to have only a single file, but diversity of entry types may make multiple files desirable, as may the pattern of updating of the file. If multiple files are to be maintained, the design must assure that users are led to the portion of the file that will serve their needs.

The major trade-off in storage media is between the ease of direct human search of the printed form and the speed of search and other manipulation in the computer-stored form. Computer storage requires a heavy investment in both hardware and software that must be justified by some combination of size, updating frequency, query unpredictability and complexity, or availability as a by-product of computer-aided indexing. As computer power becomes cheaper, and text processing systems more sophisticated, these requirements become easier to meet. Today, however, a fairly high level of use must be achieved in order to justify computer storage; even then the cost of the user's time, frequently omitted, must be included in the equation for computer search to be cost justified.

C H A P T E R 4

Alternatives in Arrangement

Introduction

Any tool that is to be used by human beings for reference rather than for narrative reading must be arranged in a known order for search. The two major means of arrangement of alphanumeric text for human lookup are alphabetical (alphanumeric) and classified. Arrangement on the basis of other graphic symbols, such as brush strokes in Chinese characters or architectural elements in slide collections, suffers from an entirely different set of complexities and is not treated here.

In alphabetical order, arrangement is on the basis of the arbitrary symbols used to express the concept; while in a classified order, arrangement is based on the internal meaning of the concepts. The notation that is the apparent basis for classified arrangement is simply assigned to the concepts after they have been arranged in the desired order.

The order used for arrangement will influence both the form of the entries made and the ease of lookup. Furthermore, as is discussed in detail later, pure alphabetical arrangement without admixture of classification, or vice versa, is quite rare, and developing the most useful arrangement requires awareness of many factors. This chapter is concerned with the options available for arrangement of files, and with the ways in which some choices affect others. Matters of entry form and access points will be considered as they affect, or are affected by, arrangement. Entry structure itself is treated in detail in Chapter 2.

While classified predates alphabetical arrangement, the latter probably is dominant today in terms of the total number of entries arranged. There has been speculation as to the reason for the change, but the exact causes are uncertain. One influence may have been the increase in popularization of learning, with more people knowing a little about a field, but not being conversant with its full detail. Furthermore, it is generally believed that in past times, fields of knowledge were both small enough and stable enough that scholars could know the arrangement of their areas and could effectively search in them, while today times have changed. Fields of learning evolve rapidly, and different people need their information arranged in different ways. This argument requires one to assume that scholars in the past saw their situations as static, with everything being known. That such a belief was universal seems open to question, because one can find complaints about rapid change and the making of too many books as far back as writing exists. The sheer bulk of material to be searched has increased, however, and this fact may be at the base of the present popularity of alphabetical arrangement.

Today, catalogues of libraries outside the Western Hemisphere are usually classified; those in the United States and Canada are alphabetical. The classified catalogues normally have alphabetical indexes, while many of the alphabetical catalogues send the user to a classified arrangement on the shelves. Book indexes are usually alphabetically arranged, while indexing services vary. If they include abstracts these are almost always arranged in a broad classified order with (ideally) alphabetical indexes; if there are no abstracts the arrangement tends to be alphabetical. Encyclopedias are often alphabetical, but may have a classified ancillary apparatus, as seen in the Propaedia volume of the *Encyclopaedia Britannica 3*. The access tools for machine-readable data bases tend to offer both alphabetical and classified means of access.

This chapter discusses the arrangement of files, whether printed or machine held, designed for human scanning or lookup. The physical arrangement of records in machine files is not considered, but the order in which they are displayed for human scanning is.

It thus considers only one major variable: whether the basis of the arrangement of the file is concepts (classified) or arbitrary symbols (alphabetical). The goal is to improve searching by:

1. bringing like items together, and
2. making the location of items within the file more predictable.

One caution is necessary here: classification is considered in this work only as a means of arrangement. While classification concepts are very important, they affect only the order of the entries in a system, so their treatment is limited to that aspect. Furthermore, the actual design and structuring of the terms is considered in Chapters 9 and 10.

Alphabetical Arrangement

In designing an alphabetically arranged file, the biggest mistake it is possible to make is to assume that filing is as simple as ABC. In natural languages based on the Roman alphabet there are at least 75 or so different characters, including uppercase and lowercase letters, digits, and punctuation marks. The alphabet and the digits each have their own generally recognized sort sequence for human lookup, but there is no universally accepted sequence when the two are combined, nor is there any sequence at all for the punctuation marks.

Furthermore, if the computer is to be used for sorting index entries (a very desirable possibility), it becomes necessary to contend with its collating sequence. Computer collation sequences bear at best a vague relationship to humanly recognized filing orders. *Government Reports Index* accepted for many years without modification a sequence that scattered punctuation marks throughout the alphabet, causing, for instance, "Johns, A. J." to file after "Johnson." All computer collation sequences separate uppercase from lowercase letters; some place digits before and some after letters (or between uppercase and lowercase); they place punctuation marks in different positions, though fortunately most place them outside the alphabet in their own subsequence. For example, in ASCII (American Standard Code for Information Interchange) the sequence is space, punctuation and symbols, digits, uppercase, and lowercase. Thus an early decision which the designer of a computer-based system must be prepared to make is the exact sort order desired for the characters in entries. This decision should be determined to a great extent by the best available knowledge of what human beings expect to find when they search an alphabetical list.

These complexities may sound at first like an argument against the use of the computer for sorting such information, but this is far from being the case. Arrangement can be made mechanical if the system is so designed. Since this is easily one of the most repetitive and mindless of chores, and therefore one highly prone to boredom-induced errors, it should be relegated to the computer. If a system is to be integrated enough really to take advantage of the capabilities of the machine, it must provide for the machine to do the filing.

About the only universal in arrangement of printed index-type tools today is the interfiling of uppercase and lowercase letters. Numerals may be filed before or after the alphabet; sometimes they are filed as though they were spelled-out numbers. Punctuation is often ignored, but sometimes it is significant.

What the designer must recognize is that the structure of entries affects their arrangement. This may seem self-evident, but often the obvious next step is not taken. If entry structure affects arrangement, then it is clearly necessary to structure the entries so that they file where it is desired that they be located.

While manual filing at first seems simpler than computer sorting, because it is unnecessary to think explicitly of sort sequences, and it may seem that one can get away with claiming to disregard punctuation, the apparent simplicity is deceptive. Manually arranged files are usually very complex because the ability of the human filer to make distinctions based on meaning is exploited. Unfortunately, there is no evidence that the distinctions made in manual systems are helpful to end users, and since these distinctions are rarely made completely explicit, it is not unreasonable to assume that the user is probably inconvenienced by an arrangement that is not self-evident.

Some rules and standards for alphabetical arrangement that may aid in understanding the complexity of the problem are those of the American Library Association (1968), American Records Management Association (1960), and the British Standards Institution (1969). The rules used by specific information services are often briefly described in the prefatory matter for their indexes. A statement of principles published in *International Cataloguing* ("Filing: Projects and Publications," 1974) was recently adopted by the International Organization for Standardisation's TC46/SC4; while general, it states some points that have not been self-evident to system designers in the past:

1. An agreed filing practice should be constructed on the basic principle of offering the most useful collocation to the most users of a particular file.
2. A standard set of filing elements should be established for each major type of filing entry, and for entries for each major type of document.
3. Entries not differentiated by this standard set of elements will be interfiled without further distinction.
4. Filing elements should be taken in the form in which they appear in the entry.
5. An agreed character sequence should apply throughout.
6. Filing criteria should be explicit.
7. Mechanisms should be established to allow agreed national filing practices, without prejudice to international exchange of records.

Agreement was not reached by the group on another proposed principle which would have required that "The sequence of filing elements within a filing field in the filing entry should be the same as their filing sequence."

Cartwright (1970) has reviewed computer filing problems from the point of view of library catalogues and provides an excellent explication of the issues.

The Sort Sequence

Many decisions about refinements of alphabetical order can be reduced to questions of sort sequence, particularly of which characters are to be included in the sort sequence, and which are to be ignored. The issues are similar whether sorting is to be done by human beings or by computers, though their resolution may be different. Only with the most primitive type of keyword system can the computer collation sequence be accepted as it stands. More sophisticated systems must use sort keys, preferably computer generated by rule or table lookup. In its simplest form the sort key table consists of a list of characters that are to be ignored in sorting, all other characters being regarded. Uppercase and lowercase alphabetic characters are always regarded, and with a few specialized exceptions, are set equivalent in the sort key. Digits are also nearly always regarded, though they may be filed before or after the alphabetic characters, and it is possible to find examples in which either arrangement will appear preferable in a specific instance.

The decision as to whether to include the space in the sort sequence or not is determined by the choice between letter-by-letter and word-by-word arrangement. If the space is included in the sort sequence it files before all other characters (in ASCII) or between punctuation marks and alphanumerics, producing word-by-word arrangement (New York before Newark). If it is ignored, the result is letter-by-letter arrangement (Newark before New York). Nearly all library catalogues and telephone books, and most book indexes, use word-by-word arrangement. Encyclopedia indexes are frequently arranged word by word but the text is usually arranged letter by letter. Dictionaries are nearly universally arranged letter-by-letter. Abstracting and indexing services vary, with firm exponents of both means of arrangement being easy to find. Thesauri, and the services which use them, are frequently arranged letter by letter. It should be noted at this point that most of the time, when the introduction to a tool states that it is arranged letter by letter or word by word, there is an implicit addition: "with exceptions." The exceptions are discussed in the later section on classed subarrangements.

With the rather drastic differences in location of specific entries produced by word-by-word and letter-by-letter arrangement (witness the number of words that can intervene between "cat" and "cats"), it seems strange that there has been so little research on the effect of each on the user. There has been a great deal of writing on the subject, and it is easy to find horrid examples of separations produced by the system one happens not to prefer, but there exist only three research studies that attempt to determine what users expect. Thompson (1976) found that if education college students were asked to file two title cards into an alphabetical file, twice as many first-year students filed letter by letter as filed word by word, while by their third year, presumably after more experience with library procedures, the proportions were about equal. However, about 35% of both groups were inconsistent, filing one card each way, or filed the cards under subjects or keywords from the title.

Shores (n.d.), in an unpublished study, found that children in grades three through six are better able to use letter-by-letter than word-by-word arrangements. In his study, children were required to search for 20 keywords in two lists of 510 entries each, one arranged word by word and the other letter by letter. The lists contained the same words and phrases, and were complex; that is, they were grouped around five basic words (air, black, long, new, and Washington), and most began with these words. The children found entries more quickly and with fewer errors when searching the letter-by-letter file. Interestingly enough, children in the lower grades (three and four) showed more marked superiority with letter-by-letter searching then those in the higher grades.

Hartley, Davies, and Burnhill (1981) found that when students were asked to write out words in the order in which they would expect to find them in an index, nearly half used a "concept" grouping, putting different forms of the same word together. The remainder used letter-by-letter, word-by-word, or some idiosyncratic arrangement. In another of their tests, 85% of a group of 12- and 13-year-old children used letter-by-letter arrangement.

At this time about all we can be sure of is that users do not make a consistent distinction between word-by-word and letter-by-letter arrangements, though naive users may prefer the latter to some extent. We therefore really have no way to guess how it would be best to file from the point of view of users.

Punctuation marks present a number of problems. It is conventional to state that punctuation is ignored in arrangement, but this is rarely really the case. Most punctuation may be ignored, but a specific significance is usually given to some marks some of the time. Thus, the comma may be used to set off inversions, and these may be filed ahead of phrase headings that are identical up to the position of the comma.

If this is the case, the comma is actually ahead of the space in word-by-word filing, while in letter-by-letter filing it is ahead of A. For example, in the Library of Congress subject headings, "Cookery, Swedish" files ahead of "Cookery for diabetics," while in the *Chemical Abstracts* indexes, filing is letter by letter to the comma, causing "Phenol, tris(1-phenylethyl)-" to file ahead of "Phenolene supra."

The dash may be used to set off subdivisions, and parentheses to set off modifying expressions; when such uses are present, the punctuation mark usually is intended to cause the item to file in a special place, as in most subject heading systems that have separate subfiles for subdivisions with the dash and parenthetical modifiers, as well as other subarrangements.

The hyphen presents special problems, as the commonly preferred arrangement can only be achieved by some form of manual intervention. It is normally preferred to treat the hyphen in a way that will cause the characters it connects to file in the same position as they would file if an alternate spelling without the hyphen were used. Words with hyphenated prefixes should be filed as single words, and hyphenated compound words as two words. The only way to achieve such a result automatically would seem to be table lookup of prefixes. It is probably preferable to standardize spelling, eliminating the hyphen as much as possible. This route has been followed in a number of thesauri, and most of the time the results are relatively satisfactory, though there may be a few rather odd-looking headings as a result. There is really no dilemma unless in a specific instance omitting the hyphen would look odd, and including it would cause the term to file out of the expected sequence.

Other punctuation marks can usually safely be ignored in sorting, though the period occasionally is used to set off initials and cause them to file as words. Putting spaces between the initials, with or without the periods, is a safer and easier means of achieving the same result.

A designer who decides to let the chips fall where they may must be aware of the implications of such a policy. The punctuation marks will have a position in the sort sequence unless they are explicitly deleted. If, for example, the hyphen is used as a connector in a derivative index to prevent the second word of a pair from generating an index entry, the word pair will be treated by the system, and arranged, as a different word in a different sequence from the first word alone. If the slash is used immediately after the last word to delimit the end of a string, as in many derivative indexes, that occurrence of the word will file in its own subsequence, usually following all other occurrences of the word. If this is desired, fine, but it is well to be aware of this circumstance in designing the system.

Many of the uses of punctuation in effect form classified subarrangements within the alphabetical file, and these are treated below.

Structuring Entries for Arrangement

Normally, filing is thought of as something that comes after the indexing is done; the entry is formulated, keyboarded, and then filed. While this is certainly the outward sequence of events, the intellectual procedure should place filing first so that the indexer first considers where in the file it is desirable to place a given concept, and then formulates the entry so that it will file there. The obvious example is in name indexing. The only reason to invert names to place surnames first is because we want to file them that way. Likewise, the only reason for the concept "antibiotics for use against fungus infections" to be phrased in the MeSH (Medical Subject Headings) vocabulary as "Antibiotics, Antifungal" is that the vocabulary designers decided they wanted all the various kinds of antibiotics to file next to each other, subarranged by use. While this principle may seem obvious, it is easy to find indexes where it has not been observed. A logical corollary of the principle is that, if at all possible, the entry should be structured so that it automatically files in the desired position. While it is certainly possible to teach human filers, and to write computer programs, to arrange entries in an order different from that of the characters in them, such practices have serious implications for users of indexes. If we tell users that an index is alphabetical, they should be able to believe us. If we write the entry one way and file it another it may be lost as far as the searcher is concerned. Of course, it is perfectly possible to place a reference directing to the actual location in the position where a searcher would reasonably expect to find the information, but all this does is increase the effort required of the user.

Any large or complex file containing many entries that begin with the same access point requires subarrangements. The point is that the entries should be structured to make the subarrangements obvious. Terms may be inverted in order to achieve a desired grouping; arrangements on the basis of prepositions and function words can also be made. While subarrangements can also be made on the basis of punctuation, these are not desirable since the punctuation marks do not have an accepted filing order. It is much better to make subgroups explicit by means of labeling. The report of the Working Party on Computer Filing Rules (1972) provides a very good discussion of the kinds of complex entries that may require classified subarrangements of large alphabetical files. For example, files may be subarranged to separate the same word as forename, surname, and place. Or, the presence or absence of specific elements in composite headings, such as parts of sacred books, may be used for subarrangement.

Classed Subarrangements

Practically any alphabetical file of a significant size, or with a large number of differentiated entries under a single access point, will benefit from use of classed subarrangements, as long as these are made explicit. Facet analysis is an extremely useful tool for such purposes, because it is quite logical to use facets for subarrangement.

While in most cases facets need to be clearly identified by a label such as "Clothing—by type of wearer—Boys," they can be implicit and still be clear, as may be seen from this selection of the subheadings found under the heading "Iron ores" in the *Applied Science and Technology Index*:

Pelleting
Testing
Transportation
Brazil
Canada
Scandinavia

Even here, however, if either subfile is long or the typography is not distinctive, a user may fail to note that there are two files.

No hard and fast rules are available for classed subarrangements. They should be introduced pragmatically as needed to make a long file more comprehensible.

Numerical Arrangements and Subarrangements

If a number appears in an index entry, how is it to be arranged? As a sequence of digits? As the number the digits stand for? As the written-out characters of the spoken number? Suppose the number is written out. Should it then be filed on the alphabetical characters or as a number?

While the answer to these questions is, as might be expected, "it depends," if at all possible the number should be written as it is to file. That is, if it is to file ordinally, an ordinal number should be keyed, not a written out word, and vice versa. Only by this means will the arrangement be made clear to the user.

If the number is implicitly or explicitly part of an ordinal sequence (91st Congress), it is normally filed as a number. If it represents a date, treatment varies in different systems and also according to whether or not the date represents a sequence, as for instance several conferences of the same name, distinguished by dates. When the date has this significance, it is again desirable to file it as a number. "DC-3 airplanes" could be treated similarly if the term were to be part of a sequence that would include the DC-6 and the DC-10.

This leaves such terms as "4-H Clubs," where the number does not imply an ordering. The alternative adopted for such terms is probably not all that vital; what is vital is adequate cross referencing. Either entries should be duplicated under "4" and "Four" or a reference should be made from the non-used arrangement.

The issue of whether numbers should file before or after alphabetical characters has been mentioned in an earlier section without resolution. If computer sorting is used, it will probably be satisfactory to let the computer collation sequence decide, placing numbers before letters in the case of ASCII. It is important, however, to ensure that integer numbers file as integers (e.g., 2 before 19) since a human being will read the latter of these numbers as nineteen, not as one nine, and expectations of arrangement will be according to the form as it is read. Manipulation of the sort key by a device such as left padding with zeroes will achieve this result.

The position of a numerical component in a sequence of filing elements must also be considered. It is common to file a term containing both words and numbers in an order different from the order in which they are cited. For example, in the Library of Congress subject headings, "U.S.—History—Civil War, 1861–1865" is not arranged among the subdivisions beginning with "C" under "U.S.—History", but as though the heading were "U.S.—History—1861–1865." In filing of chemical compound names in the *Chemical Abstracts* indexes, the words and affixes are arranged on before any digits. Thus the heading "Phenol,4-[bis(2-methyl-1H-indol-3-yl)methyl]-2,6-bis(1,1-dimethylethyl)" is filed as though it were "phenol, bismethylindolylmethylbisdimethylethyl 4 2 1h 3 2 6 1 1."

Subarrangement by date is very common, and quite useful in many circumstances. The date may be the period of the subject or the date of publication. The latter is often used to break down large files in library catalogues. One circumstance in which subarrangement by date is not very useful, however, is the practice common in indexes to biographies and historical works of arranging modifiers identifying historical events or periods of a person's life chronologically, without including the date in the modifier. The appearance presented is one of random order; if the user fails to guess that chronological order is present or does not know just when an event of interest occurred, she or he must read through the entire file.

Related to such practices is the practice of listing modifiers in page number order in back-of-book indexes. Such a listing requires the user to scan all the modifiers under a given main heading. The practice clearly derives from the methods used by some indexers of writing many modifiers on a single slip. Once this has been done, it is very difficult to rearrange them.

The following example is drawn from a history of gardens. It appears to combine a chronological arrangement with the page arrangement of the modifiers, but the apparent arrangement by time is accidental.

English gardens: middle ages, 105–8; Renaissance period, 143–9; 17th century, 172–5, 177; plantsmanship and market gardens, 196; picturesque genre, 233–48; transitional phase, 284–52 [sic]; plants and plantsmen, 252–7; in the U.S.A., 257–68; in France, 268–71; in Germany, 271–81; in other parts of the world, 281; 19th century advances in botanical science, 283–5, 287; rise to prominence of plant-breeding nurseries, 287–8; advances in floriculture, 295; paradise gardens, 295–312

Numerical subarrangement is a very useful device to divide a file, so long as the basis of the arrangement is made plain.

"File as if" Policies

Depending on the kind of index, several kinds of entries are candidates for a filing treatment not implied by the words they contain.

The obvious example is initial articles, which are always disregarded if they are in the language of the file, and usually if they are in other languages. (The exceptions are proper names such as cities—Los Angeles and El Paso.) Articles elsewhere in entries are normally, but not always, regarded. Initial articles are not a trivial problem in a machine file; Bourne (1975) demonstrated the problems arising with one approach in an experiment to determine the error rate if simple table lookup were employed for 93 different initial articles. He found an error rate of about 6% in a file of several hundred thousand entries, and concluded that some manual editing is required. While the problem of initial articles is greatest in title files, anything—including a title—can become a subject, and it is necessary to make provision for such entries. While the simplest solution, that of not keyboarding initial articles in the first place, will not appeal to all, it should be considered.

Another common, but not universal, practice is ignoring prepositions at the beginning of modifiers. The purpose of this policy is to produce a filing arrangement based on the first substantive word. While such arrangements can be useful, the alternative is worth examining. For instance, if a group of modifiers of heading X includes a sequence of the sort "A, of B," and another of "A, by C," filing on the prepositions may produce a desirable classed subarrangement. If prepositions are ignored, the fact should be indicated typographically by a device such as italics. Wellisch (1980a) makes a strong case for always regarding the preposition in filing.

Other words that may be ignored in filing include forenames (filing on initials only) and titles such as Sir and Madam. I object strongly to the former practice, but if it must be indulged, then a device such as parentheses around the letters being ignored will at least show the user what has been done. In the case of titles of honor, use of typographical distinctions, parentheses, or reformatting will serve the same purpose.

Characters are not only omitted; sometimes they may be implicitly interpolated, as when abbreviations are filed as though they were spelled out (St. filed as Saint—or as Street). The reasoning usually given for such practices is that the user does not know whether the word has been abbreviated or not. However, this is probably not the real issue, and we lack research that would inform us on a more important point. Does the user search on a visual or an auditory image? If a user has seen "St. Louis," as it is normally spelled, is the natural inclination to search on the basis of this image, or as the words would be pronounced—"Saint Louis"?

A similar issue arises when words spelled differently are interfiled; for instance, "M'" and "Mc" filed as "Mac"; "color" with "colour"; "Green" and "Greene." The first of these is nearly universal, with the important exception of telephone books. (Since telephone directories are probably used more by more people than any other kind of reference work, the rest of us should consider conforming to their practices.) The assumption seems to be that users will search on the basis of auditory rather than visual images when both are available. It seems unlikely that much searching is done on the basis of information that has only been heard, not written down; therefore we are assuming a preference, not a lack of information. This assertion receives added strength from the fact that initialisms are only rarely filed as though written out, even though there is very little conceptual difference between a one-letter abbreviation and a two- or three-letter one.

As noted above, there is no published research on how searchers think of such terms, and the situations here are exceptions to a general treatment of words as they appear in visual, not auditory, images. Some business systems, concerned primarily with the filing of names, do treat words phonetically, but systems using a broad range of terms from natural language do not. Yet, if we are to file "Greene" and "Green" as the same word, why not file "Quincy" (kwinsi), Ill., and "Quincy" (kwinzi), Mass., as different words, and under K instead of Q?

Lacking evidence, we should not make unwarranted assumptions about how users will search. On balance, the fewer special rules, the better. Any time it seems appropriate to file the entry as though it contained different information from that which explicitly appears in it, the designer should ask some questions:

1. If it is not to be filed on, is the item really necessary?
2. If the difference is necessary, how do we format the entry so that the arrangement is obvious to the user?
3. If it must be filed on, can it be added to the entry?

Summary

Alphabetical arrangement is not as simple as ABC, and research that would aid in making the best choices is lacking. Some kinds of tools are nearly always arranged letter by letter, other kinds word by word, but there is no hard evidence to aid in choosing between the two arrangements. In addition to this choice, the designer must decide which characters to include in the sort sequence, and which to ignore. When nonalphanumeric characters are included in the sequence it is usually for the purpose of introducing classified subarrangements, a practice that is dangerous because it may prevent the principles of arrangement of the file from being self-evident.

Entries must be structured for filing purposes, and any tendency to write entries one way and file them another should be carefully examined as to its necessity and value. While the production of information tools with computer aids has emphasized the issue of structuring entries for filing purposes, the new awareness should help us keep in mind that users also need an arrangement that is obvious.

Classified Arrangement

This discussion is limited to the use of classification as an arranging device and does not consider the design of classifications or the order of their classes.

There are two complementary ways of developing a classification: facet analysis and hierarchy development. As an explicit way of thinking about things, the latter preceded the former by a millenium or two. Most of us have heard of the Tree of Porphyry, and of the controversy over just how closely Dewey may have built his decimal classification on Bacon's classification of knowledge. Until Ranganathan developed the theory of facet analysis, it was assumed that the way to build a classification was to take the most general topic and successively divide it into its parts.

Bibliographical classificationists were continually bedeviled by the necessity of dividing a single topic by several principles; aircraft might be divided by kind of engine (jet), kind of user (military), or purpose of use (cargo); art might be divided by period (fifteenth century), place (France), style (impressionistic), medium (watercolor), or subject (religious). Thus classificationists had to decide whether to include military cargo jets with other jet aircraft, other military aircraft, or other cargo aircraft, with a similar problem for French impressionistic watercolors. There is no neat answer to the problem; the designer must try to anticipate the predominance of likely uses of the collection.

Hierarchical classifications are usually more or less enumerative; that is, they list most of the subjects for which they provide in the specific place where the subjects are to be classed. In enumerative classifications, if a new complex subject appears, it can only be classed with one of the simple subjects of which it is composed. On the other hand, in a synthetic faceted scheme only the truly new subject causes problems; in the more usual case of a "new" subject arising out of novel applications of an old one, or at the intersection of old subjects, the existing notation may be synthesized into a new number. Thus a faceted classification scheme could develop a notation for the American space shuttle program by synthesizing notations for transportation and for space exploration. Sayers (1975) provides one of the best available discussions of classification; while his treatment is specifically library oriented, it can be applied more broadly.

Facet analysis has not made hierarchy building obsolete; it has simply provided the classificationist with a new tool so that a classification may at several stages switch back and forth between division from general to specific and by facets. In agriculture, for example, the type of crops facet may be divided by individual crops and the operations facet by type of operation, permitting synthesis of notation for planting of spring wheat.

Classification as discussed here is essentially precoordinate, but it is perfectly possible to break down a synthesized classification number into its components, representing individual concepts, for postcoordinate search. If the notation is also synthetic, then such analysis is much simpler. It is, however, conceptually possible to break down, for instance, the notation of the Dewey classification for postcoordinate search. That this has not been done in operational situations is probably due to two factors: (1) the inherent difficulty and ambiguity of the process, in that the meaning of a given piece of notation is dependent on its context and (2) the general lack of interest in Dewey on the part of experimenters and in experimentation on the part of Dewey users.

Notation

Conceptually, the notation is a minor aspect of a classification, because it is simply a set of characters assigned to the classes so as to force them to file in the desired order. However, the actual situation is quite different; since no classification is ever "finished," and the notation must be searched, the design of its notation can greatly affect the usefulness of a classification. Notations may be pure or mixed, expressive or not, but it is important that they be searchable in manual systems and hospitable in all systems. Vickery (1952, 1956, 1957) has written a series of articles on notation design that is essential reading for classificationists.

Searchability requires that the sort order of the symbols in the notation be known; the needs are approximately the same as those for alphabetical arrangement, because the notation will be arranged alphanumerically. Searchability conflicts directly with the requirements of synthesis. A common method of synthesis is the use of reserved symbols, symbols that are not used for any other purpose, as connectors. The typical practice is to use punctuation marks, that have no filing order for humans. Thus the relative position of, say, the colon, the numeral 3, and the double quote will not be obvious to the user, even though the breakpoints will be clear. Synthetic classifications such as UDC (Universal Decimal Classification) and CC (Colon Classification) which use these symbols define an arbitrary order for them. There is an alternative, however, though it requires very careful design, and does not break up the notation as neatly as punctuation. The Bliss Classification, now entering its second edition, is the major example of a synthetic classification that does not use special symbols. Instead the notation is very carefully designed and allocated so that space is left for the required synthesis.

Hospitality is the ability to accept new concepts at any point without straining the notation. For instance, a notation composed of integer numbers is inherently inhospitable; no matter how large the gaps, sooner or later space to insert a new concept in the desired position will be lacking. A decimal notation can be made infinitely hospitable, though at the cost of expressiveness, while a synthetic notation can achieve great hospitality, but usually only by using symbols the filing order of which is not self-evident.

While expressiveness—meaning the same thing at every point in the classification—is a pleasant feature in a notation, it is not an essential characteristic in every instance. With more subjects requiring indication, expressiveness becomes nearly impossible to achieve without unduly long notation. As for pure versus mixed notation, the main issue is the size of the base; mixed notations are not, as has occasionally been claimed, more difficult to sort by computer. Of course, if notation is mixed, then the filing order of the different kinds of elements must be considered. It does seem probable, however, that long meaningless sequences of alphabetical characters are more likely to cause error than mixed or pure numerical notations. For a classification designed for international use, a pure numerical notation has the advantage of worldwide acceptance of its symbols. However, such a notation will also appear at first glance to be dividing knowledge up into 10 categories.

Size of Categories

The best size for categories in a classification depends on its purpose. Very broad general categories are usually considered sufficient for an abstracting service whose arrays are intended for scanning. In such a case there is a great deal of information with the entry, enough that the descriptor need not be sufficiently indicative to tell the user if the document fits the need exactly or not; this question can be answered from the abstract. For this purpose, the classes need only be narrow enough for the full array of entries under each to be easily scannable. On the other hand, if the classification is designed for specific lookup, the classes need to be quite narrow and precise, the more so if the information carried with the entry is limited. While the size of the collection certainly influences the detail of classification necessary for adequate breakdown, it is important to provide for anticipated growth; detail can be omitted in applying a classification scheme more easily than it can be added.

Alphabetical Subarrangement

When done judiciously, alphabetical subarrangement of classes at the lowest point of a hierarchy can be useful. If the designer is quite sure that no more useful principle of division is available at that level, alphabetical arrangement provides a known order with little trouble. The value of such arrangement is quite limited, however, as there is nothing logical about alphabetical order. The troubles that misuse of alphabetical subarrangement can lead to are graphically shown in the Library of Congress classification. For instance, subject bibliography in class Z is arranged alphabetically by broad subject name, and these names are those that were current about the turn of the century when this class was developed. To put "domestic economy" in a position closer to a more current name would require complete reclassification of all works on this subject. Countries, cities, and states are often arranged alphabetically. In recent years many country names have changed, producing a dilemma in arrangement. The many areas of the classification where states are alphabetical in one number and cities alphabetical in the next disperse parts of a jurisdiction. Yet at the time the classification was designed, such an arrangement presumably made sense, at least for the Library of Congress's collection.

Summary

When classified arrangement is used, the design needs to achieve a serviceable mix of hierarchical arrays and facet development. Topics need to be divided at various points in the array from general to specific and by aspects. While the only purpose of notation is to facilitate the arrangement of the subjects into the desired order, its design has a strong influence on the long-run viability of a scheme. It must be searchable, requiring a known order for the notational symbols; brevity is desirable, to reduce errors. Hospitality is also essential so that new subjects and changes in knowledge may be accommodated with a minimum of difficulty.

The Choice: Alphabetical or Classified

The ideal way to resolve the choice between alphabetical and classified arrangement for a human-searched file is to have both. Since this realistically is rarely possible in a printed tool, it is necessary to decide which of the two to make the primary arrangement. The controversy over alphabetical versus classified arrangement has raged for many years, as though it were possible to determine that one was best for all purposes. Vickery (1971) has put it aptly: "as though carpenters were arguing as to which tool could be used for all jobs—the saw, the chisel, the hammer, the plane, or whatever."

The popular mythology is that alphabetical arrangement has the benefit of being direct and not needing an index, but the disadvantage of separating related topics; while classification brings together relations, but is more cumbersome to use, requiring an alphabetical index to its topics. Furthermore, classifications are harder to keep up to date, since new topics may arise at any point, exhausting the hospitality of the notation; while with alphabetical arrangement it is simply a matter of authorizing the appropriate term for the new concept and inserting it in its alphabetical position. None of these claims is completely correct.

Classification and alphabetization both separate and bring together related topics. Regardless of conceptual multidimensionality, classification operationally is still linear in its physical collocation of related documents. Thus, classification brings together one set of relations but in the process separates others. Alphabetical arrangement does the same; if terms are inverted (Art, French), art of different cultures can be brought together, but not all aspects of a particular culture; if they are made direct (French Art) aspects of a culture can be brought together, but the different manifestations of art are separated. Of course, by duplicating entries one can have it both ways in either arrangement at considerable extra expense.

Similarly, both alphabetical and classified arrangements require indexes in the sense of guides to effective use. A syndetic structure may be seen as a kind of index to the index, guiding the user from the term by which the system was entered to the location of that concept in the system. Classifications require separate indexes, while the "index" can be integrated into the alphabetical system. But the most effective use of an alphabetical array also requires some sort of classed guidance, and this must be external. The separation of alphabetical and classified files is necessary because interfiling of arbitrary notations with natural language words could only bring confusion.

While the argument relative to updating may be theoretically true, actual practice is more dependent upon the policies of the organization responsible for keeping the system up-to-date. An organization that considers up-to-dateness an important goal for a classification may do a better job in this respect than one that does not consider currency important for its alphabetical system. The recent history of the Dewey Decimal Classification and the Library of Congress subject headings bears out this assertion. If the classification notation is designed for hospitality, the difficulty is further minimized.

The achievement of helpful order, and the citation order of facets, while normally discussed only in relation to classification, are not differences between alphabetical and classified arrangement. In all alphabetical index systems that use complex terms it is necessary to synthesize, and hence to select one order of facets over others. Similarly, entries are structured to achieve what is seen as helpful order, even though this terminology is not usually applied to the process. More typically the criterion is stated as in Cutter's discussion of the choice between direct and inverted order: "Enter a compound subject-name by its first word, inverting the phrase only when some other word is decidedly more significant or is often used alone with the same meaning as the whole name" (Cutter, 1904, p. 72).

Classified arrays are well adapted for scanning, or generic search, provided the arrangement of categories coincides with the user's information need, while alphabetical arrangement is useful for specific lookup of a known item or narrow subject. Scanning a classified array will lead the user to related items more easily than the cross references of an alphabetical file, since the former collocates the related entries themselves, while in the latter they are dispersed. However, for a particular, well-defined need, which the collection can satisfy precisely, it is much easier to go directly to the subject name in an alphabetical array than first to search an index for a particular location and then go to the notation in the classified array.

As noted above, the ideal solution is to have both alphabetical and classified access to a collection. In a surprising number of situations this is already the case today. Usually one of the forms has priority over the other, but both are present. The basic arrangement of most books is a form of classified order, complemented by the alphabetical index.

Most libraries in the United States and Canada shelve their books in classified order and provide an alphabetical catalogue. Libraries in Europe and Asia are more likely to use a classified catalogue, but normally provide an alphabetical index, while those in Latin America are mixed. Abstracting services are usually broadly classed, with alphabetical indexes; indexing services are generally arranged alphabetically, but many provide some sort of classified adjunct.

If the main array is to be classed, design of the alphabetical index is very important. In particular, it is necessary to consider carefully whether the class or the individual item is being indexed. If the former, the class number is the locator, while if the latter, the locator should point to the specific item—a practice that is not always observed in classified arrays. Under most circumstances, index access to both classes and individual items is needed.

For a main alphabetical array, the syndetic structure, as noted above, does serve a kind of classed index function. However, true classed access is also needed, even if only at a very broad level. Many thesauri provide descriptor group listings. These vary greatly in sophistication, from a straightforward list of all the descriptors in a group to a hierarchical array showing fairly exactly the interrelationships among individual items. Regardless of the level of sophistication, it is important that the classification be one of concepts, not of words. For example, the ERIC Thesaurus used to include in the category "Development" all descriptors containing that word; these ranged from "Behavior development" to "Site development." Such word classification does not help users locate terms of interest for a search. On the other hand, the hierarchical arrays provided in many thesauri provide a more or less well-worked-out classified arrangment of terms, even though this array is alphabetical at each level. When, as in MEDLARS, search systems provide a capability of searching on such arrays, the user effectively has the capability of performing a classified search.

Hybrids of various sorts exist. Alphabetico-classed systems enjoyed a brief popularity some years ago, and remnants of such arrangement can still be found in many alphabetical systems. In alphabetico-classed arrangement, the names of classes and subclasses are arranged alphabetically, for example,

Animals—Vertebrates—Cats
Animals—Vertebrates—Dogs

The major difficulty with such arrangement is predicting the classes and subclasses for a specific entity. For instance, in the example above, should there be intermediate steps for "Felines" and "Canids," or should the principle of arrangement be entirely different, perhaps using "Domestic animals" in the array? An alphabetico-classed system requires cross references from every step in every hierarchy—the equivalent of an index to a classification, but without the latter's systematic collocation.

Nonetheless, most alphabetical systems have alphabetico-classed characteristics, some purposeful and some artifacts of natural language. In the example used in a preceding section, inverting "Art" headings sets up an alphabetico-classed array under "Art," while entering ethnic terms directly sets up a class of ethnic features. In designing an alphabetical system, it is important to remain aware of the classed groupings one will be producing.

Another form of hybrid is the purposeful integration of classified and alphabetical arrangements, as in *Thesaurofacet* (Aitchison, 1969). In this scheme a fully worked-out thesaurus replaces the index to a faceted classification. The two must be used together, because the term relations in a hierarchy of the classified arrangement are not repeated as broader, narrower, or related terms (BT, NT, RT) in the thesaurus; the syndetics in the latter include only terms from hierarchies other than the one in which a term is located.

There are other systems, proposed and operational, for combining the production of an alphabetical and a classified array, though not normally for combining the alphabetical and classified indexes themselves. The methodology of chain indexing is based on translating the components of a classification number into alphabetical index entries, as carried out in *Library and Information Science Abstracts*. Richmond (1976) has pointed out that the Reference Indicator Numbers of the PRECIS system, by connecting Dewey classes and PRECIS terms, might make it possible to develop a system for classifying on the basis of the PRECIS terms.

Langridge (1961) has made an interesting proposal for the preparation of back-of-book indexes. He recommends that such indexes be prepared in classified order and only rearranged alphabetically when indexing is complete. Such a practice would, he suggests, improve the cross-reference structure and the treatment of compound subjects, in both cases by reminding the indexer of relationships. He does not explore the ramifications of this proposal, particularly the costs (though he appears to think the procedure might save time), but it would be interesting to see how an index might be prepared using classification as an aid.

While the main array in a printed tool will likely continue to be alphabetical or classified as a given situation seems to warrant, the trend in systems that have machine aids available seems to be toward development of hybrids in which classified and alphabetical arrays are developed from the same intellectual operation. Svenonius (1983) describes the ways in which classification may aid online retrieval from a file that is basically alphabetical. It may aid in narrowing the question by providing the general context within which a term is used, or in broadening it by substituting general for precise terms. It may also make retrieval possible in the first place by showing the conceptual context of a vague word such as "freedom."

Summary

The fundamental choice in arrangement is between the symbols used to express ideas (alphabetical arrangement) and the concepts themselves (classified arrangement). While both types have their fervent exponents, the ideal is really to have a combination of both approaches, alphabetical for the sake of the user who wants a specific topic with a known name and classified for the user who needs a survey of interrelationships or a topic that it is not convenient to name and locate in an alphabetical array.

Most alphabetical files contain classificatory elements such as inversions or categorization of entries by type, while classification schemes typically resort to alphabetical subarrangement at lower levels when there is no more useful principle of division.

In an alphabetical index the sort sequence must be determined. The letters and digits each have a generally accepted order, but there is no such order of precedence between letters and digits or for other characters. The decision on precedence between letters and numbers is essentially arbitrary, while it is best not to treat marks of punctuation as filing elements at all, since they do not have a generally accepted sequence.

The space is in a class of its own. Where it is regarded at all it nearly always precedes all other characters. The choice between regarding the space or not is a knotty one which is far from being settled. Using it means word-by-word filing while disregarding it produces letter-by-letter arrangement. Both types of filing are favored by some but what research there has been is inconclusive as to whether one is more "natural" than the other.

Arrangement is the device that makes the location of items in an index predictable; therefore, the structure of entries should be such as to cause them to file where users are led to expect to find them, rather than being of a totally different form.

In classification, concepts are arranged in a desired order, and notation is assigned in a manner that will cause the concepts to continue to be arranged in that order, whether by humans or by machines. Notation can contribute to or detract from the usefulness of classification according to its hospitality (ease of interpolating new concepts), expressiveness (consistency of meaning throughout the classification), and synthetic qualities (ease of joining concepts).

The size of the categories in a classification is typically determined by its purpose. Categories will be broad in a current awareness tool designed for scanning, and narrow in a large restrospective index.

As noted above the ideal is to have both types of array; this is frequently the case at least to some extent.

CHAPTER 5

Syndetic Structure

Introduction

The syndetic structure is the array of devices used to bring to the user's attention relations among terms that are not located near each other in the index. The syndetic structure also includes the devices employed to explain usage of particular terms in the index. These devices normally either directly or by implication also guide users to other possible terms. The scope of the term "syndetic structure" as used here is that of Borko and Bernier (1978, p. 25); it is broader than Cutter's (1904, p. 23) definition, which was limited to cross-references.

The structure is an extremely useful adjunct to index use. It is also extremely costly, since its development requires extra steps in both preparation and maintenance of the vocabulary, beyond the straightforward development and assignment of terms. It is, however, perfectly possible to design an index which has no syndetic apparatus; furthermore, use of the computer in both preparation and search of the index changes the ways in which the syndetic apparatus is developed.

This chapter will review briefly the types of syndetics that should be considered, and the factors in decisions on whether to use syndetics at all, but will pay more attention to alternatives and trade-offs in developing the structure. The pros and cons of using an entry vocabulary instead of a conventional syndetic structure will also be explored. For discussion of development of vocabulary control authorities such as thesauri the reader is referred to Chapter 10.

Before Cutter's time in the late nineteenth century, the use of cross-references and other devices to tie indexes together grew as indexing became more sophisticated, and as the need for such devices was perceived. Cutter (1904) provided a formal basis for such structures in his *Rules for a Dictionary Catalog*. He prescribed the making of "see" references downward (from broader to narrower subjects) and across (between related, coordinate subjects). An early supplement was the reverse cross-reference, used only in the subject authority list, not the index, as a record to aid in editing and updating.

Cutter's instructions governed practice for three-quarters of a century, until with the advent of thesauri in the 1950s many refinements were introduced. Under the old "see" and "see also" system, references tended to be added haphazardly; while theoretically references between broader and narrower terms were unidirectional, and those between coordinate related terms were bidirectional, the distinction often was not observed in practice. The reference structure tended to grow by accretion, with references added as the indexer happened to perceive the need. The same occurred with other devices such as scope notes. To be fair, however, a syndetic structure based on relationships observed among the information items in a collection will not in any case be identical with one based on the terms used to index those items. This conflict has never been adequately faced, let alone resolved, in index vocabulary design.

The most important refinement to syndetic structure since Cutter is the development of broader, narrower, and related term references, making explicitness of term hierarchies in alphabetically arranged subject vocabularies more feasible. This development spurred a great deal more thinking and refinement in syndetic devices but, oddly enough, little or no research. There has been no real effort to determine which, and to what extent, syndetic devices aid either indexing or retrieval. The need seems to be taken for granted, at least as far as controlled vocabularies are concerned.

The dependent variables treated in this chapter are

1. whether to use a syndetic structure;
2. complexity of the structure;
3. type of syndetics;
4. methods of showing the structure;
5. methods of developing the structure; and
6. degree of automation of structure development.

Two independent variables have a strong influence on the decision:

1. characteristics of the user group; and
2. complexity of the index universe.

The goal is to aid the user in locating information in the index, regardless of the entry point used.

Types of Syndetics

The syndetic apparatus may conveniently be divided into three types of devices: prescriptive references, optional or permissive references, and devices explaining the meaning of vocabulary terms or policies in their use. The various types are well covered in the literature (Aitchison and Gilchrist, 1972, pp. 26–38, 50–66; American National Standards Institute, 1973; British Standards Institution, 1979; Gilchrist, 1971, pp. 18–40, 66–75; Lancaster, 1972, pp. 38–69, 77–89, 121–134; Soergel, 1974, pp. 68–180; Surace, 1970), and will only be briefly reviewed here.

Explanations of Meaning or Policy

For practical purposes, the most important decision to be made regarding devices to explain vocabulary policies is the extent of use to be made of them. If there are any vocabularies with too many aids, I have never seen them; however, it is no problem at all to find the places where such aids would add to the value of almost any index one might examine. Two basic kinds of these aids are used: the note, usually known as a scope note, which explains usage of the term in an individual system; and the qualifier, usually in parentheses but sometimes in the form of an inversion, which is limited to a word or very brief phrase and is actually part of the term.

Continuing attention to provision of these aids is required. Terms are inevitably used with specialized or non-self-evident meanings in any system, and information on the use of the term in the system must be supplied to users. Furthermore, the need to keep the actual index terms terse inevitably introduces ambiguity in many cases. A note need be added only once, and it does not produce an awkward, hard-to-arrange phrase; while attempting to make the meaning totally unambiguous within the term itself could lead to real problems.

For instance, if in a particular system use of the term "Communications" is limited to the very broad, general concept, with other terms such as "Telecommunications" applied for aspects that are frequently subsumed under "Communications" in general, this guidance can most easily be conveyed in a note.

Notes may also inform users of policy changes, such as the date when a term was added or deleted or its scope changed. Searches of literature compiled over a period of time need access to this information.

Qualifiers are used primarily to disambiguate homonyms, but sometimes essentially the same information may be given in either a scope note or a qualifier. This is a rather minor choice, but it can have some interesting ramifications. Carrying the information as part of the term means repetitive keying of the information (unless terms are generated from codes), but if the syndetic structure is not included in the index, placing the information in a scope note can mean that it will never appear in the index itself, but only in the thesaurus. (See the following discussion of this choice.)

Prescriptive References

The prescriptive cross-reference may prohibit use of one term, requiring use of another for a given concept, or may require that, in some or all circumstances, if one term is used, another be used also. An example of the latter is the generic posting policy of some systems, in which documents are automatically posted to broader terms in the index hierarchy.

Failure to use such references in a controlled vocabulary system means the user receives no guidance from a term under which access is sought to the term actually used in the system. These references even have a place in searching—though not in indexing—in an uncontrolled vocabulary system: to lead searchers from terms that have never appeared in the index to terms that have.

Permissive Cross References

These come in enormous variety. Essentially, they are designed to suggest to both indexer and user that a term that is conceptually related in some way to the term being examined may be of value for indexing or searching. The relation may be between the meanings of the terms themselves or between the information items indexed by the terms.

Entry Vocabulary

The sum total of all terms and cross references composes the entry vocabulary of the index, the access points under which the indexer or searcher will find some form of guidance as to where information on particular topics is actually located.

Developing a Syndetic Structure

Whether or Not to Provide the Structure

The choice as to whether to develop some sort of syndetic structure is essentially one of costs—processing costs versus user costs. As a tool to aid users in perceiving relations that go beyond the relatively small section of the file that can be immediately seen, syndetics contribute greatly to effective index use.

However, syndetics must be learned, and the user who wants to see the index merely as a tool which is searched, under the term(s) that seem most suitable (without reference to what may be located elsewhere), may perceive them as an irritant.

If syndetics are not provided, users lack an important source of guidance, receiving little help from the index in determining where to look for related material or on the exact meaning of a particular term in the context of the index.

Thus the question, for practical purposes, becomes one not of whether to have a syndetic structure at all, but rather of how extensive it should be, the kinds of references to use, and how it should be developed. In fact, about the only type of index that frequently is totally lacking in syndetic structure is the computer-generated keyword index, and even in these syndetics tend to be added as time goes by and the need for them is perceived.

Level of Complexity

Once the decision to develop a syndetic structure is made, it is necessary to consider how complex it should be. The right level of syndetic structure reduces search effort, and once it is in place, it reduces indexer effort as well.

A wide variety of levels of complexity may be found in syndetic structures. Probably the simplest is that of the conventional subject heading system, which is normally limited to scope notes, "see" (prescriptive) and "see also" (permissive) references, and their reversals. As further refinements are developed, the single type of prescriptive reference may be refined into several, such as a simple one, another indicating that reference is made to a more general topic that includes the access concept, or yet another requiring use of two or more index terms to cover the prohibited concept. Further variations are possible.

It is in the permissive references, however, that the full range of complexity may be observed. At one end, a subject heading list may be limited to "see also" references and their reciprocals. Refinements may include distinguishing part-whole, genus-species, and other types of relations. Soergel (1974, p. 68–180) provides a very full discussion of these refinements. Graphic displays may be used to show the vocabulary in nonlinear fashion (Rolling, 1971). Permuted displays may show all occurrences of a given word in the vocabulary, while categories draw together all broadly related terms. All these devices serve in one way or another to remind the user of additional terms that may be of value for indexing or search. Most thesauri provide several of them.

All permissive and some prescriptive syndetics are recall devices; they increase recall, but at the price of some loss in precision, the amount of both gain and loss being affected by the design of the structure. It is thus perfectly conceivable that for a system whose terms were narrowly and precisely definable in terms of its literature, and where it was known that a high precision factor was to be preferred to high recall for nearly all searches, it might not be worth the cost to provide recall-oriented syndetics, though of course the ones that inform both user and indexer of where a given concept is indexed in the system would still be required. Even in such a case, however, an introductory note warning of the lack of syndetics is necessary.

Developing and Maintaining Syndetics

Developing and maintaining the structure is costly, however, and the more highly refined the relationships, the more costly. At the same time, since concepts do not fit neatly into language categories, a point of diminishing returns is certain to be reached. The precise point at which it occurs should depend to some extent on the sophistication of the user group and the degree of its dependence on the system. A highly sophisticated user group that regards the system as an essential tool will make better use of any aids provided. Similarly, the more complex the index universe, the more aids to its use should pay off in improved access. Unfortunately, the lack of research on syndetic structures handicaps the designer in determining which level will pay off best in a particular system.

For manual search, the balance of choices remains much the same as in the past, the need to provide the most precise access to information weighing against the need to avoid scattering closely related information among different terms; scattering requires both a complex reference structure and much user effort to locate the related information in several different places. The best mix can only be achieved by study in specific situations; any general rule soon turns out to have a multitude of exceptions, and/or to require so much interpretation that it is hardly a rule at all.

With the advent of machine search the rules of the game have changed. The syndetic structure can be fully or partially automated, with indexing and search performed using the words that seem most appropriate and the system translating these words into those it uses. Certain aspects of this tendency are already evident in some operations, such as those in which retrieval looks exactly the same to the user regardless of which of a number of exact synonyms (e.g., an initialism or the written-out form of a corporate name) is used. At this level, such a capability is extremely useful; it is nearly foolproof, and saves the user or indexer the chore of remembering or searching out which form to use.

As soon as this tendency is taken further, however, it becomes much more complicated, entering the area of natural language retrieval, where the structure is imposed by means of such devices as word stemming or clustering (Salton, 1975). While these techniques offer great promise for the future—perhaps even for the fairly near future—they are still highly experimental, and very few applications to indexes in operational retrieval environments have been reported. The index system designer must monitor developments in this area, in order to be ready to apply any new findings.

Choosing among Types of References

Often a scope note and prescriptive or permissive references convey essentially the same information, for example,

Communications
(limited to general works on many forms
of communications)
NT Broadcast communications
NT Telecommunications
NT Telephone systems

Here the NT references to specific communication modes could be taken to imply that "Communications" is used only for general works. A common practice is, rather than using a note, to rely on the permissive references attached to a term to indicate its scope, expecting both indexer and searcher to realize that the term is at least approximately the sum of all its narrower terms. Such a practice requires leaps of intuition that are really not reasonable to expect of searchers, though indexers presumably would master this as part of their training.

Obviously, the "choice" between prescriptive and permissive references is usually not such a choice at all; if the access term is a used one, its references obviously are permissive; if a nonused one, the references must be prescriptive. However, references under a used term may have a prescriptive component, usually as part of a note, informing the user that for some contexts or situations a different term is required.

In a system using complex terms with subheads or modifiers, a decision must often be made on whether to make a permissive reference from a main term, or to devise a nonused subhead for the purpose of making a prescriptive cross-reference from it. For instance, if all road vehicular accidents in an index are to be indexed as:

Traffic—Accidents

the designer has two choices under Automobiles (and other vehicle types):

Automobiles
    See also Traffic—Accidents

or

Automobiles—Accidents
    See Traffic—Accidents

The "see" reference from the subhead takes up more space in the index, but sometimes is best because it will be located at the point at which a user would presumably expect to find it. Using the "see also" alternative above would probably result in location of this reference among a large group of others, which a searcher looking for automobile accidents may or may not scan.

If a rule of thumb is possible, it is probably that if the subhead seems likely to be one (such as Accidents) for which a user will search specifically, a prescriptive reference from the subheading is preferable, but if it would have to be of a vaguer, less predictable nature, then use of the permissive form is preferable. For instance, a discussion of the use of the herbicide Agent Orange in the Vietnam War might be entered in any one of several places, requiring references from all the alternative locations. If it were entered under "Agent Orange," a "see also" from "Vietnam War" would probably be preferable to a "see" reference from a specific subhead, since the form of such a subhead is not particularly obvious ("Agent Orange," "Herbicide use," and "Chemical weapons" being some readily conceived possibilities).

Related to this issue is that of the choice between general ("Baseball. See also names of teams and players" or "Baseball. See also names of team and players, e.g., New York Yankees") and specific ("Baseball. See also New York Yankees") permissive references. If the general reference is chosen it is desirable to use the format that provides an example whenever either the reference or the form of entry may not be immediately obvious. In the case above, for example, the entry form could conceivably be simply "Yankees" with a parenthetical modifier.

The choice of whether to use a specific or general form should be dictated by balancing the length of the list that would be generated if the specific form were used against the likelihood that users either will not be able to think of (or search out elsewhere) all the specific cases, or will have to look in many places, only a few of which will contain entries. Long lists of specifics are costly, irritating to users, and make heavy demands of indexers and/or the system in insuring that every case is posted. General references transfer the burden to users, but insure against the misleading effect of accidental omission of one or more items from a long list.

Hierarchy Issues

The development of refinements in permissive reference structures has compelled examination of issues that either did not arise or could conveniently be ignored in the past. The most important of these are the definition of broader and narrower terms, the number of hierarchy levels to be included at any one access point, and whether a term can belong to more than one hierarchy.

Definition Issues

It is generally accepted that genus-species relationships are appropriately designated by the broader-narrower term notation, although determining what terms actually stand in a genus-species relationship to each other may not be simple for abstract concepts. The issue is not settled, however, for such relationships as that of a part to its whole. While the ANSI thesaurus guideline (American National Standards Institute, 1973) treats such relationships as related terms, many authorities and thesauri regard the broader-narrower term notation as most appropriate for this relationship, or propose use of specialized notations (Soergel, 1974). I consider the broader-narrower term relationship perfectly appropriate on the grounds that while, for example, an automobile engine is not a kind of automobile, it is totally included within the concept of automobile. In other words, any relationship that can be represented in a Venn diagram by concentric, rather than overlapping, circles, is appropriately designated as a broader-narrower term relationship. The value of adding additional types of notations has not been demonstrated, and such refinements are certain to be very costly.

Number of Hierarchy Levels at Each Access Point

The reference structure at each access point in the vocabulary may show only the next higher broader term and the next lower narrower term, or the full range of the hierarchy, or some number in between. The most important thing is that the policy, whatever it may be, be consistent. Showing the user the entire hierarchy at each access point will save paging back and forth through a file, but also consumes a great deal of space. Furthermore, the decision to produce such a listing may of itself result in a tendency to limit the length of the hierarchies developed artificially. Without some means of distinguishing the levels shown, the user is confronted by a long list of broader and/or narrower terms that may be confusing. Listing a set number of levels (e.g., two or three) up and down might be a workable compromise, but there is the risk that users will assume they have seen the full hierarchy. Given the ability to manipulate data by computer, which is so readily available today, it seems much wiser in most cases to limit the display to one level each up and down, providing a notation that leads to the position of the term in a separate display of the full hierarchy.

Terms in Multiple Hierarchies

Some vocabulary authorities today limit each term to one hierarchy of broader and narrower terms, requiring that all other hierarchical relationships be relegated to the related term notation. Such a practice simply does not conform to the way in which knowledge is organized, and furthermore, seems to serve no useful purpose. To take a simple example, a dog is a member of both the family Canidae, and the group domestic animals. Therefore, the term "dog" in a vocabulary authority should have attached to it the appropriate broader terms from both hierarchies (assuming both are used in the vocabulary). Below this level, the narrower terms will belong to only one hierarchy, of course, since all of them will represent some type, or some specific aspect, of the concept "dog."

Separate or Integrated Files

Once the decision to provide a specific type of syndetic structure has been made, the designer then must determine where to record it, whether in a separate file, integrated into the index itself, or both. In the past, existing indexing was frequently used as the authority for everything, syndetics included. Today it is common to publish a separate thesaurus containing the syndetic structure, and to provide no reference structure whatsoever in the index. And of course, there are many variants falling between these two extremes. This description naturally applies only to indexes that are serially issued or updated. A one-time production, such as a back-of-book index, will normally be complete in itself, though it is possible, and might on occasion be desirable, to index the index by providing a separate guide to it.

Today, any ongoing index system of any size needs to, and generally does, maintain a file for syndetics separately from the index; if the index is periodically produced, normally no single issue will contain the full structure. Whether the index is periodic or is continuously maintained in one file, indexers require the syndetics as part of their ongoing work, and therefore the separate file is most useful.

More open to question is the desirability (versus the cost) of providing in the index itself at least that part of the structure required by the indexing for a particular issue. Doing so increases the bulk of the index, while at the same time leading to the risk that an unsophisticated user will assume the partial structure is all that is to be found. Furthermore, when the total vocabulary, syndetic structure included, is so large that it fills an entire volume by itself, the economic argument for limiting it to a separate publication can become compelling. While the vocabulary should be dynamic, it is not nearly as dynamic as the index, and thus can be published at less frequent intervals.

On the other hand, there is much to be said for maximizing the users' convenience by making the index complete in itself. Only a very small minority of users is likely to examine a second file just to find cross-references (unless, of course, the work is online, when the frequency of use of such a file will be partly determined by the ease of accessing it). However, only a minority, but presumably a larger minority, is believed to follow up the references even when they are included in the index.

It almost certainly is not wise to reproduce the full syndetic structure in the index. A well-developed structure would overburden the index, tending to lead to limitations on the amount of structure developed in the first place. A better course is to limit the structure provided in the index to the minimum necessary for effective use of a particular issue, providing a separate tool for the full file. Hunt *et al.*'s (1976, Part 2, p. 94) findings tend to confirm this assertion, since these authors found that search precision in a PRECIS library catalogue with full reference structure was not as good as that in a catalogue whose only difference was that it did not provide a full reference structure.

If the syndetic structure is to be included in the index, the obvious question is how to go about including it once it has been developed. Naturally, only those references pertinent to indexing in a particular part of the index should be included in that part. Elements of the syndetic structure may be placed in the index automatically/clerically or manually/intellectually. A manual clerical operation is possible, of course, but is usually not worthwhile in an index large enough to warrant the use of automated procedures. If the authority file is computer-maintained, then routine parts of the structure, such as scope notes and many cross-references, can—and should—be added automatically, whether as part of a pass of the index against the authority file to check accuracy or as a separate operation. Adding routine references manually is both time-consuming and error-prone.

However, certain kinds of references require an intellectual decision on their use in a particular issue of the index, because they are justified only by the occurrence of particular information under the heading referred to. The distinction corresponds to Borko and Bernier's (1978) distinction between general and specific cross-references. A general cross-reference (in their terminology) is automatically justified by the occurrence of any material under the heading to be referred to; synonyms are the most obvious example ("Cars. See Automobiles"). Specific cross references require justification in the form of occurrence of particular kinds of information under the headings referred to ("Automobiles. See also Engines" is justified only if information pertaining to automobile engines is to be found in a particular issue of the index).

The question of whether to integrate the syndetic structure with the index in an online file is similar to that with printed indexes, but there are points of difference. The syndetic structure is usually not included within the online index, though it can be. Instead, a printed and/or online thesaurus may be made available. Lack of references in the online index causes much the same problems as in printed indexes, though in many cases online searches are more carefully planned, including search of the vocabulary authority beforehand. On the other hand, the searcher who enters a printed index with an erroneous phrasing of a term will encounter the terms that are located near the entry point; often one of these will fit the need. The user of an online file must use a special technique such as truncation to achieve the same result. When the references are included in the index file, it is possible to provide automatic retrieval of documents indexed by referenced terms. This capability is discussed in the entry vocabulary section that follows.

Means of Development

It is reasonable to divide the means of developing syndetic structures into three general categories, systematic, ad hoc, and automatic, though in real life practically all systems will use a mixture of two or even all three of these.

Systematic

Here, as the vocabulary is developed, the terms are assigned to categories, facets, and/or hierarchies and the syndetic structure is developed on the basis of these relationships. This is a highly artificial means of developing a structure because, in effect, it reflects the relations between meanings of terms, which will not coincide perfectly with the relations between documents. On the other hand, such a structure, if well executed, will have a logic of its own, and can be extremely useful.

Ad Hoc

When references are added only as the need for them is seen, each presumably serves a valid purpose, but formation of a useful network is unlikely without considerable later editing. Very careful control is required, to assure that contradictory or incompatible references are not made. Gaps are almost inevitable, particularly since reliance on ad hoc provision more or less implies that indexers are responsible for suggesting references; the extent to which needs occur to them will be strongly influenced not just by particular documents, but by their subjective attitudes at a particular time.

Automatic

This option is a relatively new one, and produces a different kind of structure from the other two. Both of the manual procedures rely on semantic relationships; while some of the relationships in an automatically generated structure may be semantic, the structure itself is usually based on co-occurrence of terms. The value of such techniques has not yet been finally determined, but it seems likely that as they are refined, it will be possible to improve their precision performance, which to date has caused problems.

Entry Vocabulary

The entry vocabulary is the total array of aids used to guide users from the terms which first occur to them for search to the terms where the information is actually located. The syndetic structure discussed thus far is one form of entry vocabulary, but another related form is taking shape in systems using advanced means of computer search. Here, much of the structure is relatively transparent to users, and the structure itself is much more sophisticated, offering more options.

Thus, automatic cross-referencing systems which switch automatically or semi-automatically from the user's entry term to the equivalent used in the system are being developed. Many online search systems use commands that enable users to view terms that are alphabetically near the search term. Clustering and automatic classification capabilities may relate user terms to other terms found in the system on the basis of statistical associations and/or semantic relationships.

Indexing systems have only begun to scratch the surface of the possibilities for guiding users painlessly from an entry point to terms where question-answering information is located. A sophisticated entry vocabulary is expensive to develop, and requires computer capabilities for search if its full richness is to be exploited. The thesaurus must not just be online, but the connections it implies must be implemented, and decisions made as to which should be automatic and which brought out for the user's consideration. Providing alphabetical lists simply requires maintenance of a list with alphabetical connections.

Developing clusters of terms can be quite costly, and is still essentially experimental.

Still open are such questions as what, if any, degree of merging of like terms will best help users and, if users are to be offered options, how best to arrange the options.

Summary

Only the very crudest indexes are produced without any syndetic structure whatever. Regardless of how user-oriented an indexing system may be, it still makes some demands on the user to guess how the answer to a query will have been expressed in a particular system. The basic purpose of the syndetic structure or entry vocabulary is to reduce the guesswork, ideally guiding users with a minimum of effort from the point at which they enter the system to the point at which the desired information is located.

Sophisticated syndetic structures are very expensive to devise, and there has been very little research on their value. Providing guidance to users seems intuitively useful, but very little information is available to guide the designer in determining which allocation of resources will produce the most useful payoff.

There are three major types of devices: prescriptive references, permissive references, and devices explaining meanings or policies in use of terms. All need to be applied in ways and to the extent that will maximize the value of the index—neither so few as to cause information to be lost, nor so many as to confuse the user.

While it is theoretically possible not to use a syndetic structure at all, only the simplest keyword indexes make use of this option, because the structure does provide an immensely useful source of guidance. The more realistic decisions are the level of complexity to be provided, the kinds of references to be used, and the means of developing the structure.

References may be limited to simple "see" and "see also" structures, or may specify part-whole, genus-species and other relationships, together with graphic or permuted displays. Costs tend to limit the complexity of the structure in any given situation, but use of machine aids does permit some kinds of references to be made much more inexpensively.

It is possible to use different types of references to convey essentially the same information; the major criterion is usually achievement of the most helpful array.

In developing the permissive part of a syndetic structure, it is necessary to resolve issues of hierarchies of terms, specifically the definition of broader and narrower terms—whether to include other than genus-species relationships; the number of levels of the hierarchy to be included at any one access point; and whether a term may be included in more than one hierarchy.

The syndetic structure may be recorded in a separate file, integrated with the index, or both. Normally a separate file for the use of indexers is highly desirable, and for the guidance of users at least part of the structure should be included in the index unless considerations of size and updating cost really dictate separation.

The syndetic structure may be developed on a systematic (relations assigned as the vocabulary is developed), ad hoc (relations added as indexers see the need for them), or automatic basis.

   Computer storage and search have enormously broadened the
range of possible syndetic structures; some new ones, such as listings
of words alphabetically near the search word, have become fairly commonplace, while others, such as the automatic clustering of terms on
the basis of associative or semantic relations, remain in the realm of
experimentation.
   The totality of access points, direct or indirect, provided in an index is its entry vocabulary; new developments in computer-aided indexing are making it possible to envision broadening the entry
vocabulary concept to the point where the difference between index
terms and syndetic structure effectively becomes transparent to the
user.

PART III

The Collection

The Collection

Introduction

The preceding part of this work deals with the subject file, or how access to a collection is organized, while the following part deals with the index term apparatus designed to provide this access. This part deals with the collection itself, the items within it, and alternatives for their treatment in the subject access system.

While any body of material to be indexed, whether a single document or a group of documents, is a collection of information or information-bearing items, there are important differences in practice between the design of an index to a collection of separate documents and one to a single document. These differences will be reflected in the discussion throughout this chapter.

It is in their treatment of the document that "indexing" and "cataloguing" have differed most, and in this chapter that the relation between the two will become most evident. Conventional distinctions present cataloguing as the preparation of lists of documents, with indexing as the provision of access to the contents of documents. Yet subject catalogues attempt to inform users of the subjects of documents—their contents—while such indexes as those to authors or report numbers, though not germane to this work, in effect provide lists of available documents.

Four variables in treatment of documents are considered here:

1. the design of a collection of discrete documents to be indexed;
2. the part(s) of individual documents that are used as the source of indexable matter;
3. the size of the unit of indexable information; and
4. the number of entries to be made for each document.

The goals are to:

1. maximize accurate retrieval; but
2. minimize the size of the index.

Design of A Collection

Oddly enough, works on indexing seem generally to take the collection as a given; that is, there is very little information in the literature on the decisions involved when an index is developed to fill an information need, rather than to provide access to a predefined body of material. Yet the scope of any collective index must at some point be defined; decisions on inclusion and exclusion must be made.

Scope

Except for the obvious influence of choice of subject matter and language limitations on the type of index vocabulary required, few of the decisions on scope influence other decisions, so the treatment here will not be extensive. The decision on comprehensiveness will influence the size of the collection and therefore of the index, but this is also a fairly obvious relationship.

The lack of attention to collection design in the literature is fortunately not generally reflected in the priority assigned to this task in the actual design of indexing services, which usually is based on rather carefully stated criteria for inclusion. This is not surprising, since any index could easily grow to be of uneconomic size. Great care is required in order to insure the most valuable index for the resources available.

It is crucial that the scope of an index be explicitly determined and that this scope be openly stated for users so that they may know the limits imposed and be able to consider whether they need to go beyond these limits.

Among the elements which should be considered in determining the scope of an index are subject, language, time period, level of coverage, and form of literature.

Subject

Nearly all collective indexes have some subject limitations because this is the main point of limitation in search needs. Obvious minor exceptions are indexes limited to time periods or languages in which there is very little material to be indexed. In such cases the period or the particular literature is in effect the "subject" of interest.

Defining subject scope is not a straightforward matter. There will usually be a fairly obvious core which should be covered comprehensively, but the exact size of the core and the means of treating peripheral subjects require definition.

Language

Unless the totality of the literature in a particular language is the actual scope of an index, ideally, language should not be a criterion at all—documents that meet other substantive criteria should be included regardless of language. Reality, however, usually dictates some limitations. Materials in certain languages are typically less available, because their physical location is remote, or users are unable to read the language, or both. They may also be hard to acquire for indexing in the first place. All these factors typically work together to result in a determination that the resources available are better expended on maximizing coverage of the literature in the readily accessible languages.

Time

This may be either time of publication, time of receipt, or, in historical works, time period covered by the publication. The latter is an aspect of subject scope and may be treated the same as other subject aspects. Time of publication or receipt is usually a criterion for issues of serially published indexes or for those which are to be updated.

Level of coverage

The audience for which an index is designed—child or adult, lay or professional—will affect both the choice of documents to be indexed and the kinds of terms used to index them.

Form of literature

Next to subject, this is probably the most typical scope limitation in indexes. Library catalogues are generally limited to books; there are indexes of reports, periodicals, and newspapers, to mention the most common. While there are some differences in the types of information to be found in the different forms of material, the primary reason for the distinction is probably tradition. Libraries catalogue their books and in earlier days catalogued the contents of their periodicals. It was early seen as economic to centralize the indexing of periodicals and the cataloguing of books, but the efforts were undertaken by different organizations and the results were published in different formats (books and cards). At that time newspapers were not seen as particularly indexable, and the report literature did not yet exist. The report literature arose under special conditions that tended to result in its continuing to be treated separately, and the sheer bulk of newspapers makes them very difficult to add to eye-readable periodical indexes.

Pre-Existing Indexes

A special case of collection design is the collecting of preexisting indexes that were compiled completely independently. Proposals to merge back-of-book indexes have been made from time to time, but they have generally foundered on the problem of the massive scissors-and-tape job that until recently would have been required. Added to this was the economic impossibility of editing the independent output of many hands into a coherent whole. Quite simply, a book index should be designed to fit its collection—a particular book. It will not fit very well a different collection—a group of books on related subjects.

Dolby and Resnikoff (1972) proposed a rationale and procedure for accumulating existing back-of-book indexes. They were able to use computer technology to edit the indexes, but had to keyboard them in order to get machine-readable copy with which to work. Kilgour (1972) is one of the books in the proposed series of CumIndexes. Only two seem ever to have been published.

Recently an effort which appears to have a much greater chance of success has been undertaken. The "Superindex" program of CRC Press has at least two advantages over earlier efforts: (1) It is intended only as an online data base, permitting more flexibility (e.g., word searching), and eliminating hard copy production costs; and (2) The indexes already exist in machine-readable form.

Unfortunately, the only available written material on this data base, which was quite new at the time of writing, was a brief summary of the results of a test of a small sample of entries (Superindex, 1982?). However, the potential appears quite promising. The file is available on the BRS online system.

Source of Indexable Matter

Indexable matter may be defined as that portion of a document from which are derived the index terms used to describe the document or its contents. While at first glance this may not seem to be a very useful concept—after all, should not the entire document be indexed?—a little reflection will show that rarely or never is the entire document really used as a source of index terms. The concept of indexable matter offers a means of formalizing and making explicit the limitations, and even of doing some research on which parts of documents are most useful as its sources.

Generally speaking, there are four major possible sources of subject indexable matter: title, prefatory matter, text proper, and end or supplementary matter. This categorization, however, masks some very significant differences, so it will be refined here to consider the following: title, abstract, other prefatory matter, headings and captions, illustrations, text proper, appended matter, and citations or references. It should be noted that not all this matter will necessarily be present for every document, and even when present it may not be physically integrated with the document. For visual and auditory material in particular, introductory or appended matter may be on the container or in accompanying documentation, not on the item itself. Books rarely have abstracts, while periodical articles may not have appended matter.

Title

The title is the first and most obvious source of index terms, and in the case of technical or scholarly material at least, if it is well written, it will contain the most important concept(s) of the document. However, the primary purpose of a document title is not to serve as a source of index terms; it is to attract the interest of readers, partly by informing them of the subject being discussed, but also by piquing their interest.

A classic example of emphasis on piquing interest at the expense of describing the subject of a technical document is a favorite of mine. A few years ago an article entitled "Apples in Spacecraft" appeared in *Science* magazine. As it happens, the article had nothing to do with apples, and little to do with spacecraft. It was a theoretical discussion of the gravitational interaction of two bodies of different size that are so far away from any other bodies that outside gravitational effects may be ignored. This title obviously piqued at least one reader's interest, but it did nothing to state the topic of the article.

Even in more conventionally written titles, it is usually not possible to express every nuance of the document without running to an unreasonable length. Thus, while the title is certainly important for indexing, exclusive reliance on it will cause useful information to be lost.

Titles of nontechnical material are even worse; the subjects will be more diffuse and harder to express precisely and in any case the motivation of piquing, as distinct from informing, will be even stronger.

Abstract

The abstract, where it exists, is, if well written, a concise summary of the major points of a document, and as such may serve extremely well as a source of indexable matter. It has far more content than the title, but is still brief enough to be scanned quickly.

However, not all documents have abstracts, and not all abstracts are well written, so the usefulness of abstracts for indexing is generally limited to documents for which they are provided, and to systems in which the desired indexing depth is such that the abstract will contain all or nearly all of the essential ideas. Furthermore, a good abstract will duplicate the information in the text, so it would normally not be useful to use both as sources of indexable matter.

Other Prefatory Matter

Books frequently contain extensive prefaces, forewords, and other introductory matter. Whether such material should become a source of indexable matter should be decided on an individual basis—whether the indexing depth is such as to permit coverage of this matter, and whether it contains significant material, not duplicated elsewhere, to which access is likely to be desired.

Headings and Captions

Headings and captions are extremely useful sources of indexable matter. In a well-guided document they will provide precise indication of the subjects covered. Headings, however, are likely to be so terse that they lack meaning out of context and must therefore be supplemented by examination of the full text.

Illustrations

Illustrations vary in their significance to the text and to the index, but they should not be neglected. They should always be covered in indexes to single documents and elsewhere when the depth of indexing warrants. Technical illustrations are normally fairly straightforward but in some other kinds of works implicit subjects may be of equal or greater importance than the explicit subjects of illustrations.

Text Proper

It is the text proper to which the indexing normally leads, but this is also nearly always by far the longest part of the document and therefore the most time-consuming to index. Hence, the text proper is frequently used, especially for fairly shallow indexing, only for scanning to confirm that other sources have not omitted significant material. The type of the unit of indexable matter (see below) is also a factor here, as information unit indexing almost requires use of the full text.

Even when the text is used as a source of indexable matter, its parts may not be equal in importance, particularly in indexes to collections of documents. Such indexes typically limit themselves to reports of new findings. While this practice may serve the majority of needs, it fails to provide access to such aspects as modes of research. One report (Swift, Winn, and Bramer, 1979), on *Sociology of Education Abstracts*, describes indexing policies that provide access to these neglected parts of the documents.

Citations

Citations may be indexed for two main purposes: (1) to provide access to the work cited as a subject—that is, to what other authors have said about the work cited; and (2) as a means of indirect subject indexing of the citing document. In the first case the indexing is performed on the assumption that users desire to learn what has been said about a document in the past—the review function, in effect—while in the second, the subject of the cited work is known, and it is assumed that the probability is high that any document citing it will be on the same or a closely related topic.

Other Appended Matter

Appendixes and other such material added at the end of a document are similar to front matter from an indexing point of view. That is, the content is highly variable, some probably being the object of search and some not. If the appendixes do contain indexable material, the issue of indexing depth comes into play here as well.

Access and Cost Trade-Offs

It is intuitively obvious that as more of the document is used as a source for index terms, two things are true: (1) the better the indexing can be, in the sense that more of the ideas in the document become accessible; and (2) the more costly indexing becomes, because processing time increases with the amount of information processed, whether processing is manual or mechanical. Also intuitively, it seems certain that there is probably some balance for each system between cost and quality of access that provides the best access for the money expended (keeping in mind the fact that resources expended to index one document are necessarily not available to index another one).

Several studies bear out this assumption, at least for journal articles and technical reports. Knable (1965) compared key words in titles with those in index terms, for shallow and deep indexing and abstracting. He found 60% of the keywords present in shallow index entries (3 per document) and 93% of those in a deep abstract (50 words or less) were not in the title, with intermediate results for deep indexing and shallow abstracting.

Keen (1968) found that abstracts were better than titles for retrieval, and that abstracts and full text were about the same, though with higher recall for the latter. He concluded that indexing from abstracts was most useful, because titles were inadequate and the extra effort in indexing from full text was not worth the cost.

Feinberg (1973, pp. 37–38) summarized the literature on adequacy of titles for derivative indexing, finding them not adequate, though better for technical articles.

These studies do not, of course, account for specific indexing needs. To take only two examples, a back-of-book index for a monograph, by definition, cannot be based on abstracts (though of course a variant, using only introductions or summaries of the parts of the book, is conceivable, and might even be warranted for a few kinds of works). If the stated intent of the index is to cover all new material of a specified type (e.g., *Chemical Abstracts* indexes cover all new information on chemical compounds), then the full text must be used at least part of the time to ensure that this information is indexed.

However, for indexes to groups of relatively short documents with abstracts present, it is probably generally most useful to index from the titles and abstracts only, perhaps cursorily checking the text to insure that there are no significant omissions.

A factor to be considered is the quality of both title and abstract. The "Apples in Spacecraft" example given previously illustrates this issue. Abstracts also may not necessarily cover the content of the document adequately. The text is the ultimate authority for indexing, though of course determination of the authority for index terms will normally go beyond the text—even if only to the indexer's personal knowledge.

Citation indexing has the advantage of being very inexpensive, because it requires no intellectual analysis unless an attempt is made to verify or correct the names cited, but it is limited in its applicability to documents in which citations are present, and the diversity of motivations in citation is at least as high as that in titling. Documents may be cited because they are actually germane to the item, but they may also be cited for background, or simply for reasons of prestige or custom. Citation indexes to technical literature are unavoidably large, since each document tends to cite many others.

Type of Unit of Indexable Matter

Some indexing systems are more or less completely limited to characterizing subjects of the document as a whole. Others, fewer in number, attempt to provide access to every item of information within the document, normally requiring that certain criteria of novelty or relevance to the subject of the system be met. The former may be labeled bibliographic unit indexing, the latter information unit indexing.

A related distinction sometimes found in the literature is that between summarization—indexing the overall themes of a document—and exhaustive indexing—the indexing of subthemes (Foskett, 1977, p. 20). However, the issue of exhaustivity level is generally treated from the point of view of the number of entries. While there is obviously a relationship between the size of the unit of indexable matter and the number of entries, the relationship is not a simple one. The matter of the number of entries is treated in the next section.

Although the distinction between cataloguing and indexing is implicitly based on this distinction between bibliographic and information unit indexing, many "indexes" blur it by providing access to documents at the bibliographic level only.

A bibliographic unit, for indexes to groups of discrete documents, is normally defined as a complete book, journal article, report, etc.; but in an index to a serial collection, it might well be the serial as a whole. At the other end of the scale, a back-of-book index, which at first glance seems necessarily to be an information unit index, may be based on bibliographic units, if these are defined as chapters, sections, or other relatively discrete entities.

Most back-of-book indexes provide access at the information unit level, but nearly all indexes to collections of discrete documents are limited to the bibliographic unit level. Chemical Abstracts indexes, with their coverage of new chemical information throughout the document, are an outstanding exception to the latter generalization.

However, the choice between bibliographic and information unit indexing is present for any type of index, though the impact of the decision will vary with the kind of collection involved. Also, it is immediately obvious that information unit indexing should be both slower and more costly than bibliographic unit indexing, since the indexer must examine the entire document to detect indexable information, rather than simply finding the answer to the question, "What is this document about?"

The bibliographic units in a typical monograph will be small enough that the search for information units will not automatically require a great deal more depth of indexing, hence the result that even low-quality book indexes are typically information unit indexes. Furthermore, a book is usually a relatively small collection of information, meaning that an index at the information unit level will not necessarily encounter serious problems of complexity.

On the other hand, an attempt to index a very diverse collection, such as the books in a general library, at the information unit level, would run into enormous problems. The cost would be very high, in itself making such an index impractical, but there are intellectual and theoretical problems too. The very diversity of such a collection means that the same information will be presented repetitively at different levels of both quality and sophistication. Furthermore, a wide variety of different subjects will be covered from different points of view. For practical purposes it would be nearly impossible to design indexing criteria, and actually impossible to apply them, to permit selection of information units and their organization into an array that would satisfy users' needs. There is no way to design an effective index without at least a general sense of what will be included. The sheer size and diversity of a library collection effectively preclude achievement of such an overview at the information unit level.

In between the single book and the library collection, effective choices theoretically are possible, even though in actuality so few resources are typically devoted to indexes that only bibliographic unit indexing can be achieved in any case.

Even in an information unit index it is never desirable to index literally every item of information. In a periodical article, well-known facts are typically presented as part of the introductory material; indexing these would add a tremendous amount of bulk without an equivalent increase in the amount of new information. Hence *Chemical Abstracts*, the best-known journal index to use information unit indexing, indexes only new information of interest to chemists. In indexes

covering "softer" subjects than chemistry, or those which are more selective, it can be much more difficult to decide what is "new" or meets
other similar criteria for selection.

As another example, it is usually necessary to assume that all information in a book must be indexed, because books emphasize synthesis more than reporting of new information. However, prefatory,
introductory, and summary sections in a book generally repeat information provided in more detail elsewhere within the work; indexing
the repetitive information is normally not helpful.

The smaller and more intensively used the collection is expected
to be, the more likely it is that information unit indexing will be both
worthwhile and affordable.

On the other hand, if information unit indexing for individual bibliographic units is already available, it will generally make most sense
to provide only bibliographic unit access, forcing the users to go to the
individual items for information unit access, rather than duplicating
the indexing. Of course one might take exactly the opposite position:
if information unit indexing for the individual bibliographic units is
available, why not merge it into a large information unit index covering
many bibliographic units? Atherton's Subject Access Project (Gratch,
Settel, and Atherton, 1978) did just exactly this, taking terms from tables of contents (bibliographic units) and from indexes (information
units) for books and merging them into a single machine-searchable
file. The CumIndex (Dolby and Resnikoff, 1972) and Superindex (1982?)
concepts are similar, except that they are nonselective and merge only
the index terms into a printed book and an online database, respectively. The problems of merging pre-existing indexes are covered in
Chapter 5; it is sufficient to note here that such efforts have not had a
great deal of practical impact on the way collections of documents are
indexed. Certainly minimizing the number of lookups is desirable, but
factors of cost and compatibility limit the extent to which this goal can
be achieved.

It is intuitively obvious that information unit indexing provides
better but more costly access than that limited to the bibliographic unit,
but the matter has never been studied in this form. It is not even mentioned, in these terms or any others, in the two major texts on indexing
(Borko and Bernier, 1978; Collison, 1972). Thus, there is little basis other
than the designer's intuition for a decision as to the relative merits of
information unit and bibliographic unit indexing in a particular situation. There is, of course, some evidence regarding the effect of the
number of entries on retrieval; this is treated in the next section.

Number of Entries per Document

If a book is taken as a single document, then obviously the possible range in number of entries per document is from one to thousands. However, the range for the choice in a particular system is much more limited. A system covering many thousands or millions of separate documents cannot—and should not—index them all at the same depth as a system covering only one. Dolby and Resnikoff (1972) (summarized by Kilgour, 1972), using index size, which certainly correlates with number of entries per document, offer an interesting theoretical explication of the various levels of indexing. They suggest that information, from the within-book level to the catalogue or index covering a many-document collection, is condensed in a ratio of 30 to 1 at each stage from full text to index to table of contents to title. Similarly, the ratio of the length of an abstract to that of its article is also 30 to 1. The amount of access clearly decreases as the level increases.

While a major purpose of their argument is to make a case for providing cumulated indexes to books, it also provides a useful aid to understanding the place of various types of indexes. Thus, the index to a book is the first level of access to it, and a catalogue listing many books by subject is at a higher level (but not the next higher level if the 30 to 1 ratio is observed). The designer needs first to consider where in this hierarchy of levels a particular index is intended to stand.

The work reported by Mischo (1979) is a clear example of the implicit use of this hierarchy of levels. The access provided to a library's reference collection by its catalogue was found inadequate, so deeper indexing of the contents of the works was carried out to provide the level of access needed for the library's purposes. This level clearly comes somewhere between that of the library catalogue and the individual, uncumulated, book indexes.

Another example is in the Subject Access Project, described by Gratch et al. (1978). In this project, directed by Pauline Atherton, index and table of contents entries meeting specified criteria were added to the MARC records of book titles, making the words in them available for machine search. Retrieval, and presumably ability to exploit the collection, were significantly improved.

Montague (1965) found that for chemical patents, indexing to a depth of 70 to 90 terms per document could produce a 90% recall level for this type of material.

Once the determination of the level at which it is intended to operate is made, the tougher issues must be faced. One, two, or ten entries per document will leave it at approximately the same level in Dolby and Resnikoff's formulation, but the amount of information—and in particular, the number of different topics brought out—will vary tremendously.

Seely (1972) reviewed six studies of the effect of indexing depth (treating depth as synonymous with number of entries). All the studies verified that there was an inverse relationship between recall and precision. As the number of entries increased, recall improved and precision deteriorated.

Clearly the type of item being indexed has a significant effect on the number of entries required to provide access at a given level. While there may not be much relation between the length of a document and its nature in the sense of how many different topics it covers, the longer document will almost unavoidably develop its arguments further, provide more examples, and generally give more information to which later access might be needed. While there is no research on the subject, this can be verified empirically by comparing a textbook on a subject with a popular article intended to provide a cursory view of the same subject. Both presumably take the individual with no knowledge of the area and teach that person something about the subject, but the resemblance in terms of need for access provision stops there.

However, the relation between document length and number of possible index entries is far from linear. Different subjects and modes of treatment affect the number also; for example, a historical treatment of a subject, covering many individuals' contributions, will generally require many more entries than a theoretical treatment of the same subject. Of course, documents vary in the number of entries required to produce the results intended for the system. Bird (1974) found that, within a given system, the number of entries per document followed a mixed Poisson distribution.

Maron (1979) showed that there is no single optimal indexing depth (a measure that is similar to the number of terms per document) for a collection of documents, that in fact the amount of indexing required is determined by the document itself.

The Trade-Offs

The design of the collection will have a significant effect on the other factors, though not in the sense of a trade-off. First comes the determination as to what material should be indexed; the other decisions about the indexing are then affected by this first choice, but they normally do not feed back to affect it. A large diverse collection of works that generally have their own indexes will normally be best covered at the bibliographic unit level, while a small, homogeneous collection needs information unit indexing. If the access tool for the collection is intended to facilitate finding of specific facts information unit indexing is likewise necessary.

There is an obvious trade-off between cost and number of entries per document, since it takes more time to generate the additional entries and more space to store them. Furthermore, the increased cost of generating additional entries is certainly not linear. Probably several entries can be generated in little more than the time required for one, but at some point the additional time required to generate another index entry may be expected to increase sharply, as the indexer must examine the document more thoroughly to detect minor but useful ideas. The increase in space required to store the additional entries is affected by a number of other factors, and is treated in Chapter 11.

The source of index terms has an obvious relationship to the type of unit of indexable matter in that, by definition, if indexable matter is drawn only from the title of the work, the index can only be at the bibliographic unit level. On the other hand, information may be drawn from other parts of documents, including the text, for either bibliographic or information unit indexing. As a similar limitation, a one-entry-per-document index can only be at the bibliographic unit level, but at the several-entries-per-document level either type of unit may be the basis. Above some indefinite number of entries that will vary depending on the type of document, indexing must be at the information unit level. If the size of the eventual index is severely limited, bibliographic unit indexing is really the only option since this unit must be covered in any case, and the information unit level almost unavoidably implies a large number of entries.

Summary

Decisions regarding the design of the collection and treatment of the documents affect the overall structure of the index and how well it serves the needs for which it is designed.

Sometimes the collection is a given, but frequently the indexer needs to consider what the criteria for inclusion should be. Subject, language, time period, level of coverage, and form of literature are all factors to be considered, though their relative importance varies in different situations.

Indexable matter may be drawn from the full text or from titles, abstracts, prefatory, and/or appended material. The purpose of the index is normally to provide access to the contents of the text proper, but the text is also the most voluminous and therefore the most expensive to index. The other resources serve to summarize the document in one way or another and the narrative ones are frequently adequate as sources of index information. Titles, however, have been shown not to be adequate except at the most minimal level.

Most indexes, with the exception of those for individual books, provide access to bibliographic units as a whole rather than to specific items contained within those units. Cost has as much to do with this as desirability, but there are kinds of indexes which should provide access only at the bibliographic unit level.

The number of entries per document is a factor of both cost of developing the index and the types of documents covered. Up to some limit, deeper indexing can provide improved access without a linear increase in cost, but the increase in both access and cost will reach a point of diminishing returns. The location of that point, however, is ill defined.

PART IV

Terms

Term Source: Internal or External

Introduction

Part IV considers the alternatives available in structure and use of terms, starting with the source from which they are derived. The selection of the source is so fundamental that this part is organized around that essential decision. The choice, aside from having major impact on other decisions relating to index terms, may also have a greater influence than any other decision on options in other areas. The choice itself is the subject of this chapter, while Chapter 8 discusses the options available for systems limited to terms found in the documents themselves (derivative indexing) and Chapters 9 and 10 discuss those for systems permitting assignment from an external source (assignment indexing).

This decision on the source of terms is basic to all other decisions on the development of an index term vocabulary, and also strongly influences the choices to be made in structuring it. For instance, if the index terms are to be derived from the documents themselves, then choices such as those between popular and technical terminology simply do not exist—the terminology of the document is the terminology of the index. Furthermore, a truly derivative index will not impose a structure on the terms from outside, limiting such an index to much simpler structures than may be developed with a controlled vocabulary.

Following a brief historical perspective, the characteristics of the two forms of term acquisition are compared and findings regarding retrieval quality analyzed. The chapter concludes with an analysis of the choice between derivative and assignment indexing.

Only one variable, the source of index terms, is considered in this chapter. There are two fundamental goals: (1) to allocate effort between input and output in such a way that the total effort is minimized, and (2) to minimize the effort required to retrieve useful documents.

Historical Background

Labeling them "derivative" or "assignment"—or even "indexes"— may be a little far-fetched in today's context, but it is still interesting to note that the earliest known surrogates, or document listings, were essentially derivative in nature, being based on titles or on initial words of the text when titles were not available. Almost as early was the grouping of documents into broad classes, however.

Crestadoro in the mid-nineteenth century proposed permutation indexing, and the "schlagwort" or "catchword" concept began to be used in German libraries at about the same time. Nonetheless, in the eighteenth and nineteenth centuries, as indexes became more common, there was a gradual but uneven trend toward use of assignment indexing. For example, in the last half of the nineteenth century, while published library catalogues often used controlled vocabularies, Poole's periodical index used catchwords from titles. The difference in this specific case at least may probably be ascribed primarily to the means of support; entries for Poole's index were prepared by volunteers who selected the index words and provided bibliographic data. Presumably the resources to develop, maintain, and encourage the use of a controlled vocabulary were not available.

Manual keyword indexing has continued right up to the present day in situations where the perception was that resources did not permit, or the intensity of use require, the development of a vocabulary for assignment indexing. However, throughout this period there has been a continuing trend toward more, and more highly refined, vocabulary control. Although this trend has certainly not been reversed, the development of automatic keyword indexing in the 1950s produced a type of index that, while it is related to earlier derivative indexes, is really a different kind of tool. The method makes possible a variety and speed that were inconceivable in the past.

In earlier derivative indexes, a human being selected one or at most a few keywords from title or text to provide access; in present-day KWIC and similar indexes, a stoplist of prohibited terms, or a dictionary of acceptable ones, is developed, and a computer is used to provide access to each of the other words in the title (or, in databases, in the full text of the machine-stored document, which today is usually but not necessarily an abstract). The large number of access points provided in these indexes was inconceivable in earlier systems. Many such derivative indexes have been developed, resulting in two parallel lines of development: human-produced assignment indexes and computer-produced derivative indexes. In recent years the trend has been to try to provide the advantages of assignment indexing by adding control devices to derivative indexing systems. These devices are discussed in detail in Chapter 8.

Meanwhile, a related development is blurring the distinction between derivation and assignment. A great deal of experimentation has taken place, primarily in the 1970s but continuing to the present, in automatic indexing and natural language retrieval. These efforts are directed toward the goal of using computer manipulation techniques on natural language text to achieve a quality of retrieval at least equivalent to that provided by good manual indexing. While they do not involve the development of a controlled vocabulary of terms for assignment in the usual sense, they do use terms appearing in other documents in a collection to influence the retrieval points for a given document. This practice certainly approaches assignment indexing. However, the roots of these developments lie in derivative indexing, and they will be so treated in this work. The reader must recognize that in time the issue of whether or not human intellectual effort is applied to the individual document may become a more useful distinction than that between derived and assigned indexing.

Comparison of Characteristics

Input versus Output Effort

The basic contrast between derivative and assignment indexing is the point in the information storage and retrieval process at which effort is expended. A derivative index concentrates this effort (and cost) at the output end, while an assignment index concentrates it at input. In its purest form an automatic derivative index system requires no human intellectual analysis of individual items. This intellectual effort has been put into the system design, and input of items becomes a clerical keyboarding operation. Even this last step may be avoided if the data are received in machine-readable form in the first place.

A nonautomatic derivative system requires human analysis to select the terms, but this analysis is typically at a rather shallow level.

The indexer decides which words describe the document content, but need not determine their precise meaning or translate them into the terms of a controlled vocabulary.

At output, however, more effort is required to locate useful terms and sort out items of interest. This effort is required as a result of the scatter, lack of guidance, and lack of term differentiation that are typical of derivative indexing. (These characteristics are discussed further in later sections.) A searcher interested in mice must search under "mouse," "mice," "rodent(s)," "Rodentia," and possibly even under "pest(s)." Even so, any of these words that do not happen to occur in the part of the document used as a source of indexable matter will be missed.

In some derivative systems, some of the effort is shifted to the input stage, in the form of human term selection or editing to add terms from parts of the document not used for automatic derivation, and to prevent other terms that are not considered useful from becoming access points in the index. For instance, if the second word of a frequently occurring word pair is deemed not useful by itself for retrieval, it may be connected to the preceding word by a hyphen to prevent an index entry from being generated. Or, the title may be the source of automatically derived terms, but the editor may add other terms from elsewhere in the document or even outside it to bring out indexable concepts not present in the title, as when "mouse" or "mice" is added to a document to which the word applies but which does not contain an applicable word in its title. Additional effort may also be used at the system design stage to provide references between terms of similar or related meanings, such as between "rodents" and "mice."

In the assignment index, all of this effort is intended to be expended at input, as a vocabulary of permitted terms, together with indication of the relations among them, is developed as part of the system design and/or as part of the ongoing indexing process. Then a skilled human being intellectually analyzes each item to determine where in the index array it should be placed. At output the searcher need only determine under which term(s) the desired information has been placed; she or he can go there directly rather than considering all the words that authors may have used to describe the concept.

A major disadvantage in fact, though not in theory, of assignment systems is that considerable resources must be dedicated to maintenance on an ongoing basis. If this maintenance is neglected, as often happens, the system becomes less useful, while remaining just as costly—or becoming even more costly—to use. The result of lack of maintenance is that as the vocabulary grows and changes, indexing for older documents becomes obsolete; some provision for currency must be made without losing the connections between the older and newer information.

Some of the advantages of assignment indexing may be gained for derivative indexes by use of dictionaries. A list of equivalent terms may be used to translate variants to a single authorized form. Then in the initial machine processing, all occurrences of the various forms will be posted automatically to this one form, that is, "mice" may be posted to "mouse" or vice versa. Even though this procedure is automatic, it is still a form of assignment indexing, in that the words of the item are no longer the sole source of terms. However, the assignment still depends upon the words, rather than upon the implicit concepts that a human indexer may detect.

BIOSIS maintains such a capability on a retrospective basis for its machine-searched files (Lefever, Freedman, and Schultz, 1972) but has not applied it to its printed indexes. The automatic edit routines for the printed Permuterm Subject Index include merging of synonyms, primarily variant spellings (Fenichel, 1971). Feinberg (1973) has described many of the devices and procedures used at input to overcome some of the disadvantages of derivative indexing.

Subarrangement Possibilities

Not every index requires meaningful subarrangements; there is a benefit only when there are a significant number of entries under a single term. The point is to save the searcher from having to read through every entry under a main term. Thus the subarrangement must be obvious and must produce a grouping which for at least some users approximates the specialized areas of their needs. However, even when a listing must be scanned in its entirety, subarrangement may be of some help if it is designed to speed perception of the meaning of the entry. While nearly all indexes provide some subarrangement under the main term, these arrangements vary in value.

It is extremely difficult to provide much subarrangement in a derivative index, because in present-day operational systems the index term is generally a single word or at best a brief phrase. Typical derivative indexes are subarranged on either the word following the entry word or an accession number. Neither of these is of much use to the searcher in avoiding the necessity for scanning a long list. Even in cases where the word following the entry word is a useful subarranging element, there is no assurance that this particular word will be the same in each case, meaning that the entire array must still be scanned.

A. Not Subarranged

marks upon the northern Mexican populations / Revision of the	49:23
marks upon the northern Mexican populations / Revision of the	49:51
w species from Durango, Mexico / *Coryphantha cuencamensis*, a n	52:183
w species from Durango, Mexico / *Coryphantha grandis*, a ne	50:134
ra de Parras, Coahuila, Mexico / *Coryphantha laredoi*, a new sp	50:172
yphytum of Isla Cedros, Mexico / *Dudleya pach*	53:132
pecies from Nuevo Leon, Mexico / *Echeveria lilacina*, a new s	52:175
ica, a new species from Mexico / *Echeveria prolif*	50:289
uthern San Luis Potosí, Mexico / *Echinomastus laui*, a new spec	50:188
nsis, two new taxa from Mexico / *Mammillaria oteroi* and M. pen	47:94
Echeveria from Nayarit, Mexico / New	51:207
ew species from eastern Mexico / *Sedum burrito*, a n	49:243
ew species from Oaxaca, Mexico / *Sedum macdougallii*, a n	49:39
pecies from Nuevo Leon, Mexico / *Turbinicarpus gracilis*, a new	48:176

B. Subarranged by taxon within country

Mexico
  Baja California revisited, 48:3, 51
  Killing and curing: succulent use in Chitipa, 48:190
  Sonoran Desert, 53:246
  Succulents of San Luis Potosí, 52:40
Coryphantha
  C. cuencamensis, a new species from Durango, 52:183
  C. grandis, a new species from Durango, 50:134
  C. laredoi, a new species from Sierra de Parras, Coahuila, 50:172
Dudleya
  D. campanulata, a new species from Baja California, 50:20
  D. pachyphytum of Isla Cedros, 53:132
Echeveria
  New *E.* from Nayarit, 51:207
  E. lilacina, a new species from Nuevo Leon, 52:175
  E. prolifica, a new species, 50:289
  E. pruinina, a new species from Chiapas, 53:292
Echinomastus
  The genus *E.* in the Chihuahuan desert, 47:218
  E. laui, a new species from southern San Luis Potosí, 50:188
Mammillaria
  M. oteroi and *M. pennispinosa* var. *nazasensis*, two new taxa, 47:94
  M. tayloriorum, a new species from San Pedro Nolasco Island, 47:173
  Revision of the U.S. taxa of the *M. wrightii* complex, with remarks upon the north-
    ern Mexican populations, 49:23, 51
Sedum
  S. burrito, a new species from eastern Mexico, 49:243
  S. macdougallii, a new species from Oaxaca, 49:39
Thelocactus
  The genus *T.* in the Chihuahuan desert, 49:213, 266
Turbinicarpus
  T. gracilis, a new species from Nuevo Leon, 48:176
  T. laui, a new species from San Luis Potosí, 47:116

C. Subarranged by province or region within country
Mexico
    Echeveria prolifica, a new species, 50:289
    Mammillaria oteroi and *M. pennispinosa* var. *nazasensis*, two new taxa from Mexico, 47:94
    Revision of the U.S. taxa of the *Mammillaria wrightii* complex, with remarks upon the northern Mexican populations, 49:23, 51
    Sedum burrito, a new species from eastern Mexico, 49:243
  Baja California
    Baja California revisted, 48:3, 51
    Dudleya campanulata, a new species, 50:20
  Chiapas
    Echeveria pruinina, a new species, 53:292
  Chihuahuan Desert
    Genus *Echinomastus*, 47:218
    Genus *Thelocactus*, 49:213, 266
  Chitipa
    Killing and curing: succulent use in Chitipa, 48:190
  Coahuila
    Coryphantha laredoi, a new species from Sierra de Parras, 50:172
  Durango
    Coryphantha cuencamensis, a new species, 52:183
    Coryphantha grandis, a new species, 50:134
  Isla Cedros
    Dudleya pachyphytum, 53:132
  Nayarit
    New *Echeveria*, 51:207
  Nuevo Leon
    Echeveria lilacina, a new species, 52:175
    Turbinicarpus gracilis, a new species, 48:176
  Oaxaca
    Sedum macdougallii, a new species, 49:39
  San Luis Potosí
    Echinomastus laui, a new species from southern San Luis Potosí, 50:188
    Succulents, 52:40
    Turbinicarpus laui, a new species, 47:116
  San Pedro Nolasco Island
    Mammillaria tayloriorum, a new species, 47:173
  Sonoran Desert
    Sonoran Desert, 53:246

Figure 7.1 Comparison of derivative index entries with (B, C) and without (A) subarrangement.

    In assignment indexes, on the other hand, structures may be developed at will to achieve any subarrangement desired under a main term. Figure 7.1 illustrates a section of a KWIC index to titles, and the kind of subarrangement possible by a simple reformatting of the same index information into two different heading-modifier formats. It demonstrates that subarrangement may improve grouping, even without going beyond derived indexing.

Scatter

The degree to which the same or closely related concepts are dispersed into different locations in an index is an extremely important aspect of quality, but the idea of scatter is poorly defined, and is therefore impossible to measure except in very general terms. While essentially everyone agrees that entry of different items under exact synonyms represents undesirable scatter, the extent to which closely related concepts should be brought together is a matter both of opinion and of the scope of an individual index. For instance, information on book publishing and periodical publishing should probably be brought together in an index to physics information, but separated in an index covering information science.

However, even with the difficulty of definition it is obvious that scatter in a derivative index that does not regularize terms must be greater than that in an assignment index. No assignment index of any quality will separate "mouse" from "mice," for instance, but such a separation will be routine in a derivative index. Such scatter requires the searcher to think of all possible variants and related terms. Even if a reference structure is provided in a derivative index to aid in finding variants and related information, the user still must search the various locations where the information is to be found.

Speed of Production

Derivative indexing is inherently faster, since the step of intensive human analysis of the individual document is bypassed. Naturally, if keyword selection is performed manually, or human editing of input is added to the system, some of this advantage is lost, but the procedures will still be simpler and faster.

Costs

While assignment indexing, because of the use of trained human indexers, is usually considered much more expensive than derivative indexing, we do not really know which type or variant of a type is more costly from the point of view of the total system. Assignment indexing, if well done and carefully maintained, puts most of the costs at the input end, where they are highly visible. A great deal of professional time goes into developing and maintaining the vocabulary and its associated syndetic structure, and then each document is analyzed individually by a human being who assigns index terms. New terms must likewise be added to the vocabulary by humans, preferably after careful analysis to determine their suitability and their place in the structure. At output, to use the system effectively, a searcher must learn how the vocabulary is structured; once this is done, a search is a matter of selecting the term(s) most suitable to a query.

In contrast, a purely derivative index is extremely inexpensive at input. Terms may be selected automatically or clerically, according to carefully designed rules. These rules in fact are the only part of the system that is costly in terms of professional human time. Once they have been developed their application is straightforward. However, at output the searcher must consider all the words which may have been used to express the desired concepts and then must scan all the entries under each search term. The modifications of derivative indexing considered in Chapter 8 change the balance of these tasks in varying degrees toward the balance to be found in assignment indexing.

While input costs can be quantified with a little effort, it is more difficult to quantify the cost to searchers and to the organization or to society of having to work harder to find information, let alone the cost of not finding it at all. Even if an approach is made to the quantification of such costs, they frequently cannot or will not be included in the cost of the system at budget time; it thus becomes impossible to make a realistic judgment as to the cost and benefit trade-offs of a more expensive input system versus presumably lower costs at output.

Even considering only input costs, the use of manual keyword selection and/or human editing will make the cost advantages of derivative indexing less clearcut, because the expensive machine processing remains, while some human costs are added. Campey (1974) has analyzed costs for various modifications of title derivative indexing. She found that tagging and editing of titles took very little time, but enrichment required nearly as much time as assigning controlled headings. Use of all three processes consumed nearly as much human time as the slowest of controlled indexing alternatives. Furthermore, computer running costs increased with more complex forms of input.

Size

Derivative indexes tend to have more entries than assignment indexes covering the same number of items, but this is by no means necessarily or always true. Derivative indexes are generally based on stoplists, meaning that entries will be generated for most of the words in the indexable matter, while most assignment index systems place limits on the number of entries generated for a typical item. However, derivative indexes may use dictionaries of permitted terms, rather than stoplists of prohibited ones, causing them to be smaller; while some assignment indexes, particularly postcoordinate ones, permit a large number of entries for each item. The actual size of an index is affected by factors other than the number of entries, such as the amount of information provided with the entry, or the format of the information. While these factors are often associated with one or another type of index, they have little necessary logical relation. Nonetheless, assuming equivalent numbers of documents are covered, the typical derivative index will be larger than the typical assignment index.

Currency and Accuracy of Terms

Stoplist-based derivative indexes automatically include very current, even ephemeral, terminology, since they exclude only words that have already appeared in the literature with such frequency and in such contexts that they are known not to be useful for retrieval. Dictionary-based derivative indexes do not have this advantage; procedures to flag new items and add them to the dictionary are necessary, and there is likely to be a lag of time between the appearance of a term in the literature and its use in the index.

It is an unfortunate characteristic of controlled vocabulary systems that they tend to develop a momentum of their own, together with a set of procedures that makes addition of new terms cumbersome, thus slowing modification of the vocabulary. Even if procedures are kept flexible, it simply is not worthwhile to integrate a term that appears once, and may never appear again, into the complex syndetic apparatus of a controlled vocabulary. Adaptations permitting limited use of uncontrolled terms are possible, however, and are often used. Terms used under such provisions tend to suffer all the problems of lack of control found with derivative index terms. In a stoplist-based derivative index, a new term will appear simply because it is not on the stoplist; whether it ever turns up again or not, the document using it will always be retrievable by the term. In a sense, currency of terms is the complement of scatter: an index that places a high value on currency will tend to permit scatter of closely related concepts under new and vogue terms, while one that values minimal scatter will tend to find a place for new concepts within the existing scheme.

Similarly, derivative indexing does not interpose the judgment of an indexer between searcher and author. The latter's words will be transmitted more faithfully in the derivative index. Whether the meaning is also transmitted more faithfully than in assignment indexing depends on a number of other factors, chief among them being the skill of the assignment indexer and the suitability of the vocabulary to the subject on the one hand, and the degree to which the author has made certain the words on which derivative indexing is based (e.g., title) accurately reflect the content of the work on the other. This currency and faithfulness to authors' words also increase scatter. If no device is used to tie the new term to more conventional ones, the content will in time be lost if the new term does not gain acceptance; if it does gain acceptance, searchers will not be led to related material predating use of the new term.

Guidance to Users

There is no inherent difference between derivative and assignment indexing in the amount and quality of the guidance they offer to users. It is equally possible with either type to develop syndetic structures and instructions for use. However, a great difference typically exists in fact; it is readily explained by the different allocations of effort. Provision of user guidance requires a significant investment at the design and development stages, but also a lesser ongoing cost at the input stage. It is the input stage to which assignment indexes allocate significant resources and derivative indexes do not.

Ease of Learning the System

Effective use of any kind of index requires that its characteristics be learned. The types of learning required for derivative and assignment indexes are quite different. It is probably easier to get something from a derivative than from an assignment index without really learning how to use it, because with the high degree of scatter in the former, the chances are good that, at any point where the searcher starts, some information will be present. Using such an index effectively, however, requires that the vocabulary of the discipline be mastered and long lists of possible terms developed. It will also, for a complex query directed to a large index, require development of strategies such as locating the same document under the terms for more than one simple concept in order to narrow the search.

On the other hand, to make effective use of an assignment index
requires the user at least to learn about the index vocabulary (as distinguished from the vocabulary of the field) so that it may be used effectively to locate the information that is present. This difference is
confirmed by Hunt et al.'s (1976, pt. 2, p. 94) finding that recall in a
KWOC (Key Word Out of Context) library catalogue was better than
recall in one using a controlled vocabulary (PRECIS or Library of Congress subject headings) for first-year university students, but that this
advantage had disappeared by the third year. For a postcoordinate index the techniques of term coordination must also be learned.

Balanced against the ease of finding something in a derivative index without preparation, once the scheme of an assignment index has
been learned effective use can be relatively simple. Assignment indexing can offer predictability. Assuming the vocabulary is well designed
and maintained (characteristics that are not automatically present), all
information on a single concept will be gathered together under a single term, rather than scattered under all the terms that may have been
used to label the concept. Furthermore, guidance from prohibited terms,
and to terms labeling related concepts, can be present.

Retrieval Quality

In the 1960s and early 1970s a great many studies were performed
in an attempt to determine if derivative indexing, nearly always on the
basis of titles at that time, was equivalent in quality to assignment indexing. Usually comparisons of recall and precision were used for this
purpose, and human assignment indexing was taken as the standard.
There was essentially no effort to decide what was "good" indexing,
independently of the type being compared. Thus, these studies were all
handicapped from the beginning in their attempt to demonstrate the
value of derivative indexing. They had to try to surpass the qualities of
assignment indexing without any real opportunity to demonstrate
unique advantages for derivative methods.

Feinberg (1973, pp. 37–42) has reviewed a number of these studies,
all of which have various problems of methodology or interpretation.
The most fundamental problem was in the definition of an equivalent
term, some authors accepting broad generic terms as equivalent to a
term for a specific concept. It was clear throughout the studies, however, that the researchers took for granted the need to search under a
great many more terms for each concept in the derivative index. They

also made no attempt to go beyond the access term in the analysis; that is, the ability of an assignment index to provide useful subarrangements was not taken into account.

Feinberg did find a general consensus that technical documents typically had more useful titles. Sometimes "technical" was defined as hard sciences, but a better delimitation was the character of the document itself: if it was on a precise technical topic in its field, the title tended to contain the requisite terms. All the studies she summarized were based on limited samples and therefore their conclusions must be viewed with some caution.

More recently a study comparing use of controlled (PRECIS and Library of Congress subject headings) and derivative (KWOCed titles) indexing for library catalogues (Hunt et al., 1977) found controlled and derivative vocabularies similar in recall and precision. While the study by Hodges (1983) is not reported in enough detail to permit solid conclusions, it does indicate that the situation has not changed dramatically. She found that about 50% of the items listed under the subject headings in a search contained a word that was part of the search request.

The major conclusion one must draw from most of these studies is that the observers were examining different phenomena. There is no other way to account for findings that show derivative systems retrieving anywhere from 30 to 98% of the relevant documents that the assignment system used for comparison retrieved (Yerkey, 1973). One does gain a clear impression from these tests that it is generally not possible to achieve with derivative indexing from titles a quality of retrieval equivalent to that of assignment indexing from larger sources of indexable matter. Even to come close requires considerably more effort at the output end in such tasks as searching word variants. There is no guidance whatever on whether the lower quality might still be cost-effective in some situations.

In general, human assignment indexing was taken as the standard in these studies; the goal was to test derivative indexing against it. Thus, none of the tests directly measured quality of indexing; objective standards were and are lacking, so the best that could be done was to compare the new method with the old one. Feinberg (1973, pp. 22–24), in summarizing the literature on consistency of human indexing, shows that it is not an appropriate standard—though of course consistency is in itself no guarantee of quality.

Borko (1964) approached the question from a different point of view. Rather than comparing retrieval quality, he compared consistency of indexing between humans and between humans and machines. He found that, using a task requiring classification of documents into 11 categories, human reliability was .870, while the correlation between computer and human was .766. The clear implication is that in this limited situation at least, computers may be only slightly poorer than humans.

DeJong-Hofman (1978) found that in machine search of the INSPEC database the number of free text terms required for full coverage of concepts was quite large and cumbersome; this researcher expressed concern that retrieval failures might be caused by failure to consider all possibilities.

Hamill and Zamora's 1980 study was considerably more limited and practical in its goals than its predecessors. They ran a series of tests to determine if titles could be used to assign documents to the correct abstract classification in *Chemical Abstracts*. Matching word occurrences against probabilities determined for human-classified documents (i.e., using human assignment indexing as the standard), they found that 78% of the documents were assigned to the correct one of the five section groupings, and that 67% of the individual section assignments, including cross references, were correct. These results are good or bad depending on one's point of view. They assume the human assignment was "correct"—and being based on the entire document it certainly has a better chance of being correct. However, at the rate of 100 document assignments per second, the automatic method is presumably cheaper. Certainly the use of derivative techniques for assignment at this gross level is promising enough to warrant further study. An interesting sidelight on the issue was provided by Gifford and Baumanis (1969) who found that user relevance judgments were correlated with frequencies of words or word groups.

Choosing between Derivation and Assignment

While derivative and assignment indexing are used for the same broad purpose—to locate information—the ways in which they carry out this purpose are so different that it probably is not realistic to attempt to decide if one is "better" than the other without qualification. It all depends on the balance of needs of the system. Lancaster (1972, pp. 220–222) has summarized some of the trade-offs. He points out the effect of input and output volume: it is better to expend resources at the end of the system that experiences the heaviest load, so that a system making heavy use of a small number of documents should allocate more resources to input, while one making lighter use of a larger number of documents may well economize at input even though this means more effort at output. Similarly the requirement for speed of input (e.g., current awareness) versus speed and accuracy of output (e.g., poison information) may determine where the effort should be concentrated.

Finally, the form in which information is available as a by-product may make it worthwhile to use it in the form in which it was originally prepared. The present author would submit, however, that this last alternative should only be employed if the index is not worth producing in itself. If the index is of sufficient value that it would be justifiable to prepare the information for this purpose alone, then the fortuitous availability of the data in less than the most useful form should not be allowed to prevent modification to make the database more useful.

It should be evident by now that the ideal would be not to have to choose at all, to be able to search an index by either natural language (derivative indexing) or assigned subject terms. Henzler (1978) proposes this as an ideal, showing that neither free text search nor assigned indexing is adequate alone. The dual capability is rapidly becoming fact for machine search, if not for printed indexes, as many databases produced as by-products of printed indexes are searchable by both text words and assigned index terms.

In fact, the INSPEC service provides three kinds of access: a classified arrangement of abstracts, controlled vocabulary indexing, and free language for machine search. Field (1975) reports on a test designed to determine if the controlled vocabulary and classification could be derived from the free language terms. He found a coincidence of 70% (approximately, depending on treatment of partially correct and doubtful assignments) between machine and manual assignment of index terms, compared to coincidence between human indexers of 85%. Classification was not as satisfactory, particularly for one-place-per-document assignments. Costs, however, were found to be comparable.

A trend in this direction is also becoming evident in full-text newspaper databases. The full text by itself is often found wanting and there is a trend to addition of indexing terms derived from a small controlled vocabulary (Perez, 1982).

The combination of derivative and controlled search is available on a very limited basis in most of the printed indexes which are based on rigidly controlled thesauri. Such systems usually permit use of noncontrolled terms that may be derived from the document to supplement the controlled terms. Extensive use of free terms in conjunction with controlled vocabularies in printed indexes is unlikely however; the cost of producing hard-copy documents imposes too rigid a limitation on the amount of access that can be provided.

A factor to consider is the extent to which assigned indexing actually differs from derived indexing, for if there is little difference, then the choice should be determined by cost, and would normally favor the derivative process. The studies summarized by Feinberg (1973, pp. 37–42) and other more recent ones attempt to approach the question, but in fact confound the difference by making no attempt to deal with issues of scatter or vocabulary structure. One point of vocabulary control is to save users from having to search under all the diverse terms that authors may have used. Furthermore, few large indexes are confined to keywords; yet these studies usually neglect the contribution of phrases, modifiers, subheadings, etc., to retrieval.

Williams (1974, pp. 233–234) reviewed the literature on the value of including title words in a machine search along with index terms, and found the answer to be database-specific. Titles are useful additions in some databases but not in others. Overall, she found as might be expected that adding more access points raises recall and lowers precision. As noted earlier, the terms of this debate may change in the future too, if it becomes feasible to use computers to assign index terms, rather than just to derive them from the text.

Summary

While in many present-day situations it is becoming possible to provide both derived and assigned indexing, it frequently is necessary at least to decide the relative allocation of resources between the two.

Assignment indexing concentrates effort at the input end by providing for analysis of individual documents and their placement into an array that can be carefully structured to reduce output effort. Derivative indexing minimizes input costs at the price of increasing output effort to search in every place where the words used in natural language to describe a concept might fall and to sort out a large number of entries under keywords. Thus the density of use expected is a good guide in the choice: if heavy use is to be made of a smaller number of documents, effort should be concentrated at the input end; if use density will be lower, it may be more economical to use derivative indexing, concentrating resources at output.

Derivative indexes can be produced faster; if user or search costs are ignored, they are cheaper. It is not known under what circumstances they may be cost-effective if user or search costs are included. They tend to be larger than assignment indexes because most are based on stoplists, generating an entry for every word not on a list of prohibited terms. Derivative indexes will be more faithful to the author's terminology and will tend to contain more current terms, but they are dependent on the words that happen to be used in the document, meaning that connections between closely related concepts may be missed. It takes less learning to get some results from a derivative indexing system, but effective use of an assignment indexing system can be easier once it has been mastered. While assignment indexes typically provide more guidance to users, this is not necessarily the case.

The jury is still out as far as quality of retrieval is concerned; it all depends on how the measurement is made. The question may become moot in the near future because developments in automatic document analysis may make the important question not whether indexing is assigned or derived but whether it is human- or machine-assigned.

Derivative Indexing Alternatives

Introduction

Early in the development of indexing, and again in the development of KWIC indexing, it was recognized that words other than those
of the text might be useful for retrieval. Fischer (1966) documents the
early years of KWIC indexing and its variants. Tools usually considered
to be indexes, as distinguished from concordances (which this book
does not treat), are selective; they do not provide access on the basis
of every word in the text. The purpose of this chapter is to examine the
choices in these two areas: which words to include in indexing, and
ways in which the words may be modified or supplemented while
maintaining most of the benefits of automatic derivation. Computer-
based indexes will dominate this discussion because they dominate the
field.

The following variables are treated in this chapter:

1. degree of objectivity in selection of terms,
2. use of word inclusion or word exclusion criteria,
3. use of characteristics of the collection,
4. modification of terms,
5. amount of machine use,
6. format, and
7. subarrangement.

The goals are to:

1. use machines effectively,
2. minimize the number of useless entries,
3. maximize the number of useful access points,

4. minimize size of the index,
5. reduce human intellectual effort at input,
6. minimize scatter, and
7. use current terminology.

Term Selection Choices

Subjective or Objective Means

Subjective means of term derivation are exactly what the name implies: a human being examines the document and selects terms she or he considers useful for retrieval. This selection method was the basis of the original Uniterm system, and it is still used in installations where the indexing process is entirely manual and clerical. It is rarely used in automatic systems, however, simply because if the data will be machine processed anyway, the computer may as well generate the index entries also. It will make all the entries a human would make and more. Of course, not all of the additional entries will necessarily be useful, but their cost in computer processing and printing is relatively small compared to the cost of having humans select the terms.

Stoplist or Dictionary

This choice may also be regarded as one between negative and positive selection, since use of a stoplist permits all words not found on it to become index entries, while when a go list or dictionary of permitted terms is used, only words actually appearing on the list may generate entries.

Stoplists are much more commonly used than dictionaries in machine-based derivative indexes, probably because they fit the basic assumptions of this form of indexing so much better. A stoplist requires only the recording of a few tens to a few hundreds of common words (though occasional lists are larger), while a dictionary requires careful analysis of the universe of documents before indexing begins to try to determine all the words that should be permitted as index terms. It is, in fact, a form of vocabulary control device.

Unless provision is made to alert a human to new words (requiring the equivalent of a stoplist of known words in addition to the dictionary), the dictionary will quickly go out of date as new terms enter the vocabulary of the field. Not being in the dictionary, these will not generate entries. The *Bibliography of Agriculture* uses a dictionary for its printed version. All words are passed against the machine-stored thesauri (one for primary and one for secondary terms) and only those that are in the appropriate thesaurus can generate index entries.

On the other hand, a stoplist, if its size is to remain manageable, will inevitably let pass many terms that are not of indexing value in a particular instance. The result is to increase the bulk of the index. Longer stoplists require more processing time, while the additional words will occur relatively less frequently, so that each successive word added to the stoplist has less effort on index size than its predecessors, while costing about the same to process. Feinberg (1973, pp. 48–58) found that a stoplist of 16 words removed 29% of the words from a sample of titles, while one of over 1500 stopped 48% of words. Lists of intermediate size, ranging from 150 to 600 words, stopped from 31 to 39% of words. Thus, once the very high frequency, nonuseful words are stopped by a brief stoplist, a much longer list is required to have a significant effect on the size of the index.

On the other hand, at least one major data base service vendor has toyed with the idea of doing away with stoplists for computer search on the grounds that even words like "A" or "I" are used with a precise, searchable meaning in certain contexts. For instance, "I" is the chemical symbol for iodine. Obviously the user would have to limit searches on such terms much more strictly than when using more conventional terms, but they would have their value where Boolean search is possible. While enlargement of the machine-held index would certainly be costly, the database service does not have to face the same bulk of paper and ink that the hard copy index producer must consider. Nor is shelving or filing space at a large number of locations an issue. The index to the database would simply contain more pointers. Including such terms in a precoordinate printed index would be useless, since there would be no effective way to select out the few useful occurrences from the overwhelming majority of valueless ones.

Various refinements of stoplists may be used, the main one being multiple lists. These are found primarily in systems that generate word pairs for indexing. The words on one list are prevented from indexing at all; those on another may be prevented from appearing in the lead position, but be permitted as secondary terms. Garfield (1976) gives a useful description of the application of the two-stoplist concept to the *Permuterm Subject Index*. Words such as "behavior" and "method," which are used too often to be of value by themselves, still may aid in making another term more precise and may thus be valuable as secondary terms.

Another type of list contains words that are stopped unless they appear in conjunction with specific other word(s). The cost trade-off in using more than a single stoplist is essentially that of more complexity in computer programming, and of course the concept is only applicable if some form of word pair generation is being carried out.

While dictionaries are rarely used in typical derivative indexes, they have found an application in various forms of machine-aided indexing. Klingbiel's system (Klingbiel, 1973; Klingbiel and Rinker, 1976; Burress, 1980) at the Defense Documentation Center uses what amounts to a dictionary. Phrases are generated and processed against a list of approved terms; matches become index terms. Those that fail to match either the dictionary or a stoplist of prohibited terms are listed for human consideration, thus minimizing the problem of a dictionary's inability to pick up new terms.

Document or Collection Characteristics

All indexing is obviously based on the characteristics of the document and of the collection, since its goal is to provide guidance to the information contained within them. This discussion covers more formal use of such characteristics in index term derivation.

Derivation of index terms from text on the basis of characteristics, primarily various frequency measures, of the document or the collection is carried out almost exclusively in machine search systems, not printed indexes. Such work is primarily experimental, but there seems to be no inherent reason why, if term selection by such criteria turns out to be of value for machine search, it could not also be adapted to printed indexes. In fact, the decision on adding words to the various vocabularies and stoplists of the *Permuterm Subject Index* is strongly influenced by frequency data gathered for this purpose (Garfield, 1976).

Typically, terms that occur at middle frequency ranges—that is, neither extremely often nor extremely rarely—are chosen as index terms. In other situations terms may be clustered into groups on the basis of their co-occurrence, with retrieval based on membership in a cluster. Sparck Jones and Salton have been two of the most active workers in this area; some of their work is cited here (Sparck Jones, 1973, 1976; Salton and Wong 1976) to illustrate their efforts. While the use of techniques to permit selection of terms on some basis more sophisticated than the simple fact that they occur at all would be desirable, operational testing has been lacking, and there is no way to guess how well experimental work would scale up to the operational level.

Furthermore, Kim (1982) found that relative frequency of scientific words, as measured by their inclusion in the *Thesaurus of Engineering and Scientific Terms,* did not conform to a Zipf distribution, showing a low type-token ratio. Words in the *Political Science Thesaurus* did exhibit a Zipf distribution. There can be as yet no final interpretation of these findings because thesaurus language is not natural language and words could not be expected to follow the same frequency distribution.

Van Rijsbergen (1978) has provided a useful tutorial on methods of automatic classification of terms based on characteristics of the collection.

Some caution is warranted in application of frequency-based methods for derivative indexing, however, because Weinberg (1981) has found that the words used in human indexing do not conform to the expected pattern. In tests based on the full text of 65 articles in the field of engineering, she found that the words selected by four different indexing systems could be of high, medium, or low document or collection frequency. Since the four systems (author indexing and three published services) were reasonably diverse in their design, their indexing is probably a reasonable representation of the words that might be useful for retrieval. If further research bears out these results, the entire conceptual base of frequency-based methods will have to be reconsidered.

Choosing a Term Selection Method

The discussion above shows that there are several aspects of this choice:

1. between subjective and objective means;
2. if objective means are used:
   a. among stoplist, dictionary, or a combination,
   b. size of list if any, and
   c. whether to develop multiple lists; and
3. whether to attempt to use characteristics of the document and/or of the collection.

In choosing between subjective and objective means of term derivation, the choice essentially comes down to the amount of machine aid available. Even though most machine-derived indexes will be bulkier than most human-derived indexes, the extra cost normally will not compensate for the time and cost—and unreliability—of having humans select the derived terms. If machines are not available, the situation is obviously different, and this fact will force the use of human means. The difficulty is that if the selection is done subjectively—that is, without a set of computable rules for the human to follow—it will suffer the worst inconsistencies of reliance on text words without the compensating advantage of the consistency and speed of computer selection.

In operational systems today the opportunities to use characteristics of the collection in derivation of terms on an ongoing basis are limited, but this will not be the situation for the indefinite future, and the designer should consider whether enough of the material is available in machine-processable form, and whether computing capacity is also available to make it feasible to apply some of the findings of research on clustering and weighting to the indexing process. It is rarely feasible to keyboard large bodies of full text, as distinguished from titles, for the sole purpose of machine search. In the meantime, frequency data are of great importance in updating dictionaries and stoplists.

Lists of permitted and/or prohibited terms are the typical devices used to permit selection of terms by objective means. Only in highly specialized situations such as some concordances is it worth the cost in space to provide access to literally all the words in the document. It is worth considering, however, whether in a collection designed for Boolean search the extra access might be worth the extra cost. The answer will almost certainly be negative unless the collection is machine-stored; in this case it is worth looking at the possible specialized meanings of common character sequences to determine if the same access can be provided by other terms. For example, in the case above, is the "I" for iodine the only means of access to this concept in certain documents, and if so, would enrichment (discussed later in this chapter) still be cheaper than providing the extra machine storage?

Assuming that some form of list will be used to limit the number of terms for which access points are generated, a variety of choices is available. The fundamental one is between stoplist and dictionary. A dictionary is most feasible when space is limited and resources are available to maintain it. If space is less limited, or the system must be more or less self-maintaining, a stoplist is a better choice, accepting for the sake of economy of processing the useless entries that will be generated (a stoplist will be shorter than a dictionary) and the gain in access to novel terms.

Once a few very common terms have been stopped, a great many more words must be added to the stoplist in order further to reduce the size of the index significantly. This is almost never worthwhile unless the savings of resources would be large—for example, many pages of printed index or a great deal of computer storage. It is practically impossible to quantify the "cost" of the relatively minor user aggravation at having to bypass lists of useless terms in a printed index, or of having to heft a heavier book, and it is probably not really worthwhile to take these elements into consideration in most cases.

The decision as to whether to use multiple lists is constrained by whether terms are to be subarranged and/or precoordinated, and is therefore treated below as part of that discussion.

Alteration of Derived Terms

Almost from the beginning, indexes rigidly limited to derived words have been found more or less unsatisfactory, and the terms themselves have been modified or new terms added. Access may be required from the second part of some compound words, while additional words may co-occur so strongly with certain other words that they are superfluous as access terms by themselves. Words may be selectively stopped manually simply because they are seen as not useful in a particular instance.

On the other hand, provision may be made for addition of terms that are not actually present in the indexable matter, a process known as enrichment. While term hyphenation to prevent indexing, and splitting to add it, may be performed automatically, enrichment is essentially manual.

This section will emphasize title derivative indexing, because indexes derived from larger bodies of data such as abstracts or full text have less need of intervention to alter access point provision, and hence less of such activity takes place.

The range of procedures is enormous. At one end of the spectrum an editor may glance quickly at each title to confirm that it is reasonably indicative, adding a word or two if it is not. At the other, a wide range of human and machine editing processes may be used.

Enrichment may be simple and ad hoc, as noted above, or it may be a process nearly as complicated as conventional assignment indexing. The system used in the BIOSIS indexes is perhaps the best example of the latter. In addition to ad hoc enrichment, this service consistently provides a wide range of specialized access points, such as the phrases "new genus," "new species," etc., for every description of a new taxon.

Similarly, editing to prepare word pairs or larger word groups may be simple and ad hoc, or may be based on dictionaries and lists, being applied by computer. Such devices may serve the simple purpose of reducing the number of useless entries in the index, or may be designed to improve the structure of a precoordinate index by putting together phrases that then are indexed as one word. For instance "birth control" is such a common and specialized phrase that forcing it to be treated as a single word will make possible a useful secondary breakdown without loss of any significant access (an interest in all uses of the word "control" is highly unlikely; nor will a searcher interested in birth control search under "control"). Neufeld et al. (1974) describe the system used in the *Current Contents* weekly subject indexes, where phrases up to four words long may be generated; generation of these phrases does not depend on the original word order.

Likewise, in word pair indexes (later discussed under "Formats") two or more stoplists may be used, one of words that may never be used for indexing, and another of words that are prevented from becoming access points, but which are permitted to appear as secondary terms. Such a procedure allows terms that are useful only in limited contexts to appear in those contexts and in no others.

The ultimate in alteration of derived terms, of course, is the substitution of another term, typically from a thesaurus. While strictly speaking this is a form of assignment indexing, it is being treated in this chapter because the transformation is based on the words of the document rather than implicit concepts.

The simplest form of substitution is probably the merging of singulars and plurals and of word ending variants. Regularization may extend, however, to passing the terms against what is in effect a thesaurus. Lefever et al. (1972; Lefever, 1973) describe the system in use for the BIOSIS database. No thesaurus control is exercised in the printed index, but a machine file that combines synonyms and variants for retrospective search has been developed. All words appearing at more than a threshold frequency have been put in this file with equivalents to aid in machine searching.

The *Bibliography of Agriculture's* machine-held thesauri perform similar services for its printed version. Variant forms of words, synonyms, and equivalents in other languages, are all regularized to a single form on the basis of the thesauri.

Salton (1975, pp. 19–20) uses similar procedures in his automatic content analysis. Words are usually stemmed in his system, and in some versions they are passed against a machine-stored thesaurus.

Some experiments have carried this even further. Burnett, Cooper, Lynch, Willett, and Wycherley (1979) and Willett (1979) have tested the use of automatically derived character strings of either equal length or equal frequency. In the tests, based on the Cranfield collections, trigrams and the larger sets of equal-frequency strings provided retrieval quality equivalent to the words of the texts. However, these tests have not been scaled up to the operational level, so it is not known if the results would be the same in a real-life system.

Pros and Cons of Altering Terms

It is costly in machine and human processing time to add any of these refinements. Campey (1974) has shown that the cost of enrichment approaches the cost of human intellectual analysis; she has also developed data on the added cost of machine processing for longer stoplists. The savings in storage, whether machine or hard copy, of processes that reduce the number of entries may be calculated relatively easily.

Much more difficult is to determine the user costs of the various options. Is the extra cost to users of bypassing a useless or duplicative group of entries significant? Is the user cost in extra labor and/or missed information of not providing any terminology control significant enough to warrant providing such control? If any control is provided, a syndetic structure leading from the synonyms and variants to the place where they have been entered is definitely required; such a structure is needed in any case.

If an automated thesaurus is used, processing costs are obviously increased, while user time and costs are saved; but there is also a more subtle cost in the accidental combination of homographs associated with such procedures. This writer's favorite was the entry under "Birth" of a work with "Natal" (South Africa) in its title. This item, while only a minor irritant in itself, should serve as a warning that other more serious homographs may be present. In this case, search for the document involved under the name of this South African locality was extremely unlikely, so no information was lost; it simply was located in a useless place. Careful ongoing study of terms in the universe is required to ensure against this.

It seems wisest in any case, however, to make all processing as automatic as possible in order to guarantee consistency. These indexes are highly mechanical, and their mechanical nature should be followed throughout to avoid disservice to users.

Degree of Machine Use

The extent to which machine aid is used is generally determined by the resources available and by the size of the index. It will normally not be economic to develop extensive machine aids for a small index (if the aids already exist, of course, that may be another matter), because equivalent results may be achieved more cheaply by humans if the investment in programming will not be recouped by repetitive use. If the machine resources are not available, they will obviously not be used. The computer may be used as an aid in term selection, updating of stoplists and dictionaries, updating of lists of terms to be modified, generation of phrases, and description of characteristics of the collection.

As in the work of Klingbiel on the Defense Documentation Center system previously described, the computer may provide listings of terms that meet certain criteria for the human indexer to consider. A common procedure is to develop lists of words that do not appear on the various stoplists and dictionaries in the system. Examination of these terms simplifies updating of the lists and/or addition of new terms for particular documents. If subarrangements are to be used, the computer may be used first to develop lists of words to be joined as phrases when they occur, and then to detect their occurrence and make the actual joining. The only practical way to gather data on such characteristics of the collection as word frequency is by computer; the labor involved in manual methods makes these impractical.

In summary, the computer may be used at all stages of derivative indexing, from developing and updating the stoplists and dictionaries, through the actual indexing, to detecting words for which special treatment is required. The level of use is obviously limited by the available resources, but is also limited by the size of the universe to be indexed, since it usually is not worthwhile to develop the routines for a small index, though existing routines may be used with indexes of any size.

Formats

While both derivative and assignment indexes face problems of format, certain essential differences result from the facts that the designer of an assignment index frequently has the option of arranging on subsidiary portions (subheadings or modifiers) of a complex entry while the designer of a derivative index may use the elements of text surrounding the derived terms for arrangement. Given these different opportunities, format questions are treated separately for derived and assigned indexes in this work. While the issue of format does not arise in a machine-held index, this discussion is fully applicable to the ways in which the results of a machine search are listed out.

If an index is conceived as simply a list of single words followed by locators, formatting problems are confined to a determination of whether or not to repeat the word for each locator, whether or not to allocate a new line to each locator, and how closely to space columns. The answers to such problems are fairly easy to arrive at and it is unnecessary to dwell on them.

Format becomes interesting when the index is more than a list of single words with locators; at this point it is necessary to go back to the essential function of the index for guidance. An index is intended to guide to information. Obviously, it should carry out this function as expeditiously as possible, with minimal inconvenience to users. At the same time, for the sake of economy the index should consume as little space as possible, consistent with fulfilling its function.

Adding more than a word and a locator to an entry can serve one or both of two purposes. Material for subarrangement of the file may be provided in order to make it easier for users to locate the specific aspect of a topic in which they are interested, and to give additional information about individual entries to aid users in sorting out those that are of interest to them.

The ideal is not the provision of as much information as possible; the logical extension of such a policy would be provision of the entire document with each entry—a collectanea. Rather the goal should be to provide the amount and kind of information that will permit the locating and sorting out described above. The issue of the amount of information to provide is discussed fully in Chapter 2; here are considered the problems of formatting the information provided in the way that that will best aid users.

Types of Formats

Essentially there are two basic kinds of formats for a derivative index: one (typified by KWIC) in which the access word is embedded within the context of the text from which it is derived, and one (typified by KWOC) in which it is not. The issue is not the same as whether to provide the context somewhere in the entry, but rather how to format it if the context is to be provided as part of the access point. Providing the context as part of the access point is a rather simple and straightforward means of giving some aid in sorting out information, but it limits the potential for more precise aids in subarrangement or for subsidiary terms.

In addition, if the context is to be provided in the most common way, namely KWIC, line length problems are significant. Figure 7.1A illustrates a KWIC format. If the access point is provided in the context of the information, then it is for all practical purposes necessary to limit each entry to a single line. Furthermore the use of the space on this line cannot be perfectly efficient since the accidental propinquity of words will determine which appear. In title derivative indexes there is also an issue of line length, since a short line provides less information, while a longer one will result in a great deal of wasted white space for short titles.

Formats such as KWOC in which the term is not embedded within the context line are more flexible, permitting a wider choice of how much space to allow and whether that space should be formatted in one long line or several short ones. However, these formats also require more eye movement to take in each entry. Figure 8.1 illustrates a KWOC-type format of the same entries as in Figure 7.1A. Note that this format is similar to the example in Figures 7.1B and 7.1C, except that a secondary term has not been provided. The entries in Figure 8.1 are arranged in locator order, the most common arrangement for KWOC indexes.

Mexican
  Revision of the U.S. taxa of *Mammillaria wrightii* complex, with remarks upon the northern Mexican populations, 49:23
  Revision of the U.S. taxa of *Mammillaria wrightii* complex, with remarks upon the northern Mexican populations, 49:51
Mexico
  Turbinicarpus gracilis, a new species from Nuevo Leon, Mexico, 48:176
  Mammillaria oteroi and *M. pennispinosa* var. *nazasensis*, two new taxa from Mexico, 47:94
  Sedum macdougallii, a new species from Oaxaca, Mexico, 49:39
  Sedum burrito, a new species from eastern Mexico, 49:243
  Coryphantha grandis, a new species from Durango, Mexico, 50:134
  Coryphantha laredoi, a new species from Sierra de Parras, Coahuila, Mexico, 50:172
  Echinomastus laui, a new species from southern San Luois Potosí, Mexico, 50:188
  Echeveria prolifica, a new species from Mexico, 50:289
  New *Echeveria* from Nayarit, Mexico, 51:207
  Echeveria lilacina, a new species from Nuevo Leon, Mexico, 52:175
  Coryphantha cuencamensis, a new species from Durango, Mexico, 52:183
  Dudleya pachyphytum of Isla Cedros, Mexico, 53:132

Figure 8.1 KWOC entry format.

Space Requirements

Since many more entries are generated for a given number of items in a typical derivative index than in a typical assignment index, allocating the same amount of space to each entry would result in the consumption of vastly more space overall. Depending on the mode of term selection, a derivative index may have from 4 or 6 to 10 or 20 entries per item, while it is common for an equivalent assignment index to have only 2 to 3 entries. As a result, entries in derivative indexes are typically briefer, in some styles being limited to what will fit on a single line. Clearly the number of entries trades off against the space requirements, and the final design should maximize access to the desired information, while minimizing the effort required to sort out nonuseful information.

Subarrangement

Trying to provide a useful subarrangement can aggravate the space consumption problem. As a word index, the derivative index faces the problem of arrangement under the entry word. The accident of the word that happens to follow in the text is not adequate for meaningful subarrangement; yet some subarrangement under words that may have literally hundreds of entries posted to them is certainly needed. One solution that has been used is to develop algorithms for selection of a secondary word. If the algorithm generates only one word per main word, as in the *Bibliography of Agriculture* system, then it does not affect space requirements, but if it selects several words, as in the Permuterm system or Double-KWIC (Petrarca and Lay, 1969) where every meaningful word is indexed with every other meaningful word, it will multiply the size of the index by several times. At this rate, even one line per entry will produce an extremely bulky index.

Figure 8.2 shows an example of such entries. It covers only the part of the alphabet from A to N, for about half of the titles in previous illustrations. Furthermore, some editorial decisions appropriate to the data base were made, leading to hyphenation of the phrase "new species," taxonomic names, and names of places. There are still two to three entries for each title under the main word "Mexico."

All such procedures still provide a very limited approach to the problems of structure for index entries compared with the structure available in assignment indexes. Craven (1982) describes a limited test

Mexico	
Coahuila	50:172
Coryphantha-cuencamensis	52:183
Coryphantha-grandis	50:134
Coryphantha-laredoi	50:172
Dudleya-pachyphytum	53:132
Durango	50:134
Durango	52:183
Echeveria	51:207
Echeveria-lilacina	52:175
Echeveria-prolifica	50:289
Echinomastus-laui	50:188
Isla-Cedros	53:132
Nayarit	51:207
new	51:207
new-species	50:134
new-species	50:172
new-species	50:188
new-species	50:289
new-species	52:175
new-species	52:183
Nuevo-Leon	52:175

Figure 8.2   Permutation of secondary terms in titles.

of NEPHIS (Nested Phrase Index System), a computer-aided system for automatic coding of titles for derivative index generation. He found that this system produced structured entries from titles that were satisfactory in themselves, but there is no way to guess how well they would fit into the array of a real index. The development of truly integrated structures awaits a considerable advance in the state of the art, probably in the area of linguistics, which to date has had far less impact on information science than the closeness in subject matter of the two disciplines would seem to warrant.

Relationships among the Factors

As noted above, the amount of machine aid available tends to predetermine the method of term selection in derivative indexes, since it is so easy to select objectively by computer. Furthermore, extensive computing power is required to analyze the characteristics of the collection for use in indexing.

Alteration of terms actually intergrades with subjective means of term selection, as at some point along the continuum of adding, deleting, or modifying terms one is, in effect, using subjective means of selection, rather than more or less subjectively altering the objective output.

Using automatic objective means with a stoplist tends to predispose toward use of the KWIC format for the sake of its relative compactness, though if many entries are generated by term permutation lines may be kept very short in order to permit more columns to the page (cf. the *Permuterm Subject Index*).

Summary

The designer of a derivative index system must decide whether to use subjective or objective means of term selection, that is, whether to have a human select words that seem useful or to have a human or a computer select words according to precisely defined rules. If objective means are chosen, it is necessary to decide whether to use negative (all words not on a stoplist) or positive (all words present in a dictionary) means, or a combination of the two.

If a useful subarrangement is desired, some means other than accidental propinquity must be devised. Such means typically are based on syntax or else on straightforward permutation.

Format choices are constrained by space requirements, the need for subarrangement, and the method of term selection. Use of stoplists, with the greater size this implies, requires a more concise format. If an attempt is made to make search easier by providing subarrangements, then obviously the format must make the subarrangement readily visible.

In general, derivative indexes are automatic indexes; they avoid expensive human analysis of each document, permitting greater speed and economy of production, but with limitation to explicit word expressions as the indexing source. Providing useful access to complex concepts is extremely difficult, since these may be stated in so many different ways. All derivative index systems of any size must confront this problem, even if they then simply ignore it. If, however, the problem is faced, it leads to attempts to control indexing better, by adding terms or stopping them; and to format decisions designed to provide a useful subarrangement. The logical conclusion to this trend will be the development of fully automatic indexing systems with syntactic or semantic controls.

CHAPTER 9

Assigned Terms

Introduction

This discussion of assigned term indexing systems actually covers two chapters; it is inevitably considerably larger than the treatment of derived term indexing because, once one departs from the words of the text as the source of index terms, the number of alternatives increases dramatically. The variables to be considered in development of an assigned term system may be grouped into four broad areas:

1. natural or constructed languages,
2. degree of coextensiveness of terms with subjects,
3. relative complexity of term structure, and
4. structure of the index term vocabulary authority.

This chapter treats the first three of these choices; the fourth is discussed in Chapter 10.

The goal is to develop terms:

1. whose location is predictable;
2. that are easy to learn, apply, and search; and
3. that aid in minimizing the time required to locate useful documents.

Natural and Constructed Languages

Strictly speaking, a "natural language" indexing system would be confined to the use of words and phrases to represent subjects in the exact form and order in which they would appear in normal discourse.

A constructed language would then be any other type, whether one using natural language words in an artificial order and/or form or one using a totally artificial language. However, with the exception of systems limited to single words and very simple phrases, most so-called natural language indexing systems that use term assignment do not use the terms in exactly the same format as they would appear in normal discourse.

Therefore, this discussion will be divided into four sections: artificial language, pure natural language, and modifications of natural language, concluding with consideration of the choices to be made.

Artificial Language

An index term serves two basic purposes: it describes the subject, and it provides a basis for placing entries on the subject in an index array, normally near related subjects. There is no need to develop an artificial language to achieve the first of these purposes (except in multilingual indexes), since the natural language expression of the subject will be more readily understood by users in any case.

A purely artificial language in the indexing sense is a classification notation. This is the ultimate in term assignment, since it need bear no relation to natural language. Its essential purpose is to bring out relations among terms or documents different from those that would be brought out by arranging on some form of natural language terms, whether modified or not. Classification has been treated extensively in Chapter 4 from the point of view of arrangement; this being the essential reason for choosing an artificial language for indexing, the reader is referred to that discussion for a more extensive treatment. Some aspects of design and arrangement will be recapitulated here from the point of view of the design of the language.

The designer of a classification notation must recognize and provide for the two fundamental modes of division of subjects: hierarchical (larger to smaller) and faceted (aspects). Conceptually a classification is multidimensional, but when used for arrangement it is constrained to be linear. The notation must be expandable in some fashion to permit addition of new topics in locations that allow retention of the integrity of the language itself.

Pure Natural Language

As noted previously, the index must be limited to single words and brief phrases if it is to use pure natural language in a controlled vocabulary system. Such systems are very rare, since if vocabulary control is to be used in the first place, the additional effort to reformat terms to some extent will usually be undertaken.

Many thesauri are limited to direct-order terms, primarily in a natural language form, but careful examination will usually show that for some complex concepts, a form that is unlikely to occur in normal discourse has been adopted. Some examples from the ERIC Thesaurus are:

Body Height
Administrator Attitudes
Perceptual Motor Coordination

This usually arises when the system designers quite correctly decide that certain complex concepts should be precoordinated, yet the natural language expression(s) of the concept either start with a word that is not especially useful as the access point, or have so many alternative means of expression with function words and variant word orders that a condensed form is seen as preferable.

Modification of Natural Language

All vocabulary control of multi-word terms involves selecting one phrase form from among several possibilities; therefore such systems are all constructed to at least some extent. Usually the construction is designed to cause related terms to fall together—a form of classification. Vickery (1976) shows that all forms of vocabulary control involve some classification because grouping of word forms means in effect classifying them as equivalent.

A system that uses terms from natural language is arranged on some form of the words used to express the concept. The ways in which natural language may be altered in a constructed language will be the primary emphasis of this section. These alterations fall into three major categories, though combinations of the three are common: (1) alteration of word order; (2) telegraphic style, with omission of function words; and (3) specialized syntax.

Alteration of Word Order

Essentially, this is inversion, though it may become far more complex than merely a reversal of the order of two words. In particular, phrase-type modifiers may be multiply inverted. For example, the NEPHIS (Nested Phrase Index System) can produce (Craven, 1982):

> Reference services, computer-based
> education and training for

This example is made up of title words; the vocabulary is controlled only in the sense that word order is altered. On the other hand, the indexes to *Chemical Abstracts* contain the following type of entry:

> Plasmid and Episome
> of *Escherichia coli,* drug resistance in relation to, drying of bacteria effect on

The primary purpose of altering word order is to place an entry in the physical position in the index where it is thought to be most useful, both where the searcher is most likely to look and in juxtaposition to related information—a form of classification. The matter of when and whether to invert main headings has received a good deal of attention in the literature, but very little formal study; practice in writing modifiers or subheads has hardly been considered at all.

Most of the study of phrase inversion has been from the point of view of library subject headings, and has essentially been limited to attempts to make some sense of existing practices. Soergel's (1974, p. 312) advice, while given in the context of thesauri rather than of subject headings, is typical. He limits his discussion to two-word terms in which the noun may be considered the "focus" and the adjective the specifier or "difference." He then states that "the rationale for the inverted entry is to have the focus in the first position and then give the difference." He proceeds to give some exceptions to this rule without stating why they should be exceptions. It is clear from the context, however, that in all the exceptions the noun is not the "focus," that is, the adjective actually carries the meaning, as in the phrase "organic reactions."

Milstead (1980) reports on work with the Library of Congress subject headings that showed a general tendency to prefer the word that is less common in natural language as the access point, though the decision is usually made on the basis of the noun, that is, either all of the headings containing a specific noun will be inverted or none will be; only rarely will some be inverted and some entered directly.

An example illustrating this point may be taken from the subject of literature:

> English fiction
> Hungarian fiction
> Short stories, English
> Short stories, Hungarian

Here the common form of literature is always entered directly while the less common form is always inverted, without regard to the relative frequencies of the particular national adjectives involved.

The conventionally cited instructions are those of Cutter (1904, pp. 72–75) to enter under the first word unless "some other word is decidedly more significant, or is often used alone with the same meaning as the whole name." The difficulty is with the phrase "decidedly more significant." There has been a marked tendency to treat the noun as the significant word in some cases, but not according to any definable rules. The result is that users have no reliable basis for predicting where a given subject will be located.

This is probably the essential reason for the trend today in newer vocabulary authorities toward strict direct entry, often prohibiting any inversion except of personal and some other proper names. For instance, Gilchrist (1971) never even mentions inversion as an option.

There is no denying that the essential purpose of inversion is to provide a classified type of order, presumably on the assumption that searchers will be better served. However, for every example of a need that is better served by inverted order, one may find another that would be better fulfilled by direct order. The biggest problem of inverted order is that it is unpredictable—unless of course one goes to the lengths proposed by Prévost (1946), who advocated a rigid rule of placing the noun first in all cases. While such an inflexible rule has the advantage of predictability much but not all of the time, it has a tremendous corresponding disadvantage in that many concepts will be entered where no one would normally ever look. For instance "Nations—Interrelations" for "International Relations" will not be located where users will expect to find it. If one is to adopt a rigid rule, direct entry is probably preferable, because such a rule is predictable and corresponds with natural language. However, there has been no research designed to discover which access point is better, let alone under what circumstances one or the other might be preferable.

One study, however, throws a little light on the degree to which inversion within an entry aids or hinders comprehension. Craven (1982) found that human NEPHIS coders seemed to prefer relatively shallow nesting (each level of nesting is an inversion) and suggests that less complex permutations are more readable.

Telegraphic Style

Function words (prepositions, conjunctions, articles) may often be omitted without doing violence to clarity of meaning, for example, "Fads, Hobbies, Leisure" or "Physical properties, aluminum" instead of "Fads, Hobbies, and Leisure" or "Physical properties of aluminum."

Such constructions serve a variety of purposes. They may aid in arrangement; if a function word is present in the entry in a position that would cause it to affect the filling order, then a choice must be made between filing on a nonsubstantive word or filing on characters in a sequence other than that of the entry. The constructions save space, and result in that many fewer characters for users to understand. Against this, however, there is the danger of ambiguity, and words should never be omitted if to do so reduces the clarity of the entry. Furthermore, not all prepositions will be reasonable candidates for omission, because the mind must fill in the omission and it makes certain assumptions; if the assumptions are incorrect confusion will result. The study of Raghavan and Iyer (1978), described later, found that inclusion of function words improves user comprehension of index phrases. Even if the omission will be understood correctly, it is still not desirable to be so telegraphic that the user is slowed rather than aided in scanning by the necessity of stopping to comprehend an awkward phrase. At this point the value of specialized grammar and syntax becomes apparent.

Specialized Syntax

Complex index terms normally have a specialized set of structural rules. Punctuation marks may be assigned meanings that go far beyond their significance in natural language. Terms will be implicitly rearranged in ways that can be reconstructed in much the same way as a sentence is parsed. The essence of the problem is that if a sequence of words is simply strung together without indication of their relationships, ambiguities are inevitable; therefore syntactical refinements are required.

Coates (1973) has given perhaps the best theoretical explication of the need for some kind of explicit syntactic structure in formulation of complex index terms. His discussion is in the context of systems using role structures and of the relational indicators developed by Farradane.

Much simpler than the systems that form the background for Coates's description, however, are the subheadings and modifiers used in library subject headings and in many printed indexes. Library subject headings have a extensive implicit syntax of their own. Lilley (1959, pp. 49–50) developed a transformation rule that enabled him to produce a sentence of the type "This work is about. . ." from a subject heading and its subheading(s). Almost universally he found that a subject heading transformed by his rule matched a sentence based on a description of books entered under the heading. The essence of the formula was the switching of inversions to direct order and the substitution of prepositions for marks of punctuation.

The complex inversions mentioned above are another form of specialized syntax.

Kaiser (1911, 1927) developed a semantic approach to the grammar of subject terms with his concrete–process distinction. He conceived of essentially all concepts as decomposable into things and actions, known as concretes and processes. He then required that the concrete be the access point with the process serving as a subhead or modifier. He went so far as to break down many nouns into artificial compounds—for example, "Bibliography" became "Books—Study" in his system. Prévost's "noun-first" principle, described earlier, is related to this, but Kaiser's work goes further and is more carefully developed. This work has been poorly known and has not had the impact it deserved. While the original design was oversimplified, Kaiser's insights have value today, because they may be applied in structuring complex terms.

Choosing the Means of Modification

The common theme running through all these ideas is the acceptance as a given that complex terms must be used in an index language. From this point, however, two streams of thought become evident. These streams are based on two different kinds of index format. In the one case complex terms are used in a printed index that cannot provide direct access to every part of the term; therefore the terms must be compact and searchable; in particular, the access point must be predictable. In other situations postcoordinate indexing is assumed. Here the issue is not one of access points—every word may be an access point—but one of false coordinations. Therefore the decision on the kind of modification may be affected by the system of coordination to be used. This trade-off is discussed in Chapter 11.

The choice between artificial languages and versions of natural language has been discussed in Chapter 4 in the context of classified and alphabetical arrangements; the reader is referred to that chapter because the choice is basically a matter of the type of arrangement preferred. This leaves the various types of modifications of natural language in a precoordinate index to be evaluated here.

As already noted, it is extremely difficult, if other than natural word order is used, to develop a system that will enable users to predict the location of a specific concept. Of course, a preference for "natural" word order can really apply only to simple adjective–noun phrases; even with these there may be alternative ways of expressing the concept. Such alternatives are almost always available in the case of more complex concepts.

Direct word order for natural language phrases is to be preferred for the sake of predictability unless other criteria supersede this one in priority. When a complex term is required to express a concept, specialized modifications of word order are required. The most important characteristic of any modification, whether it be telegraphic style and/ or specialized grammar and syntax, is that it be effectively transparent to users. Obviously, observant users will notice that the index terms are not pure "natural language," but they should be able to make sense of entries without learning a new set of grammatical rules. Specialized grammar and syntax make it possible to order the words in index terms in the desired way, far more compactly and often more clearly than by use of phrases with function words.

A close second in importance is that the system be easy for indexers to learn and to apply consistently, so that it will be reasonably inexpensive to operate. The predictability that helps users also helps indexers. The degree of modification required is largely determined by the complexity of the term structure, treated later in this chapter.

Coextensiveness versus Pigeonholing

This issue has appeared in many guises, important among them being the degree of specificity, and the choice between alphabetical and classified arrangement. Essentially it boils down to the extent to which the index term reflects the precise content of the item of information as compared with assigning the item to a preformed class that may or may not be reasonably coextensive with its actual topic.

The argument over specificity has centered on the claim that the index term should reflect the exact subject of the document rather than the broader class to which it belongs; on the other hand, many authors and designers of systems have called specificity "relative," stating that the appropriate degree of specificity is determined by the collection and the use to be made of it. Unfortunately, no one has ever defined the concept of specificity to the full satisfaction of anyone else, so the argument is probably literally unresolvable in the terms in which it is usually stated. The definition of "specific" in terms of a document subject may be limited to the basic concept as distinguished from its many aspects, or may be extended to cover a variety of aspects of the subject. The former view is that seen implicitly in library subject headings, in which the main term is usually a precise statement of the basic subject, but aspect breakdowns (subdivisions) are likely to be limited to pre-

defined terms designed for grouping documents rather than for spec-
ifying them. The latter view is well put by Vickery (1975, p. 8): "The
specific subject of an article is not a simple concept which can be neatly
tucked away in a single pigeonhole in the vast cabinet of knowledge. . . . It is a compound, more or less complex, of simple concepts."
No index term can be completely coextensive, for to describe literally
the entire subject of a document would require a description or series
of descriptions of the same order of magnitude as the document itself.
By definition, selection is required; the issue is how selective the representation should be.

    When the issue is considered in terms of alphabetical versus clas-
sified arrangement, it is usually on the basis of the claim that the alphabetical subject term may be devised to represent the subject exactly,
while the classified arrangement requires that the preformed "pigeonhole" closest in size to the subject of the item be used. This argument
has some validity when applied to traditional subject heading systems
and primarily enumerative classifications; the latter are composed primarily of pigeonholes while the former allow some flexibility. However, the use of synthetic features even in traditional classifications
permits the index term to become about as coextensive as desired,
while, as previously noted, traditional subject heading systems are specific only at the simple subject level, not at the level of the aspect.

    Speaking in terms of the operations of real-life systems, at one end
of the spectrum is the kind of index in which a degree of specificity is
used that will uniquely distinguish each item from all others in the index, as in the indexes to *Chemical Abstracts*. At the other end are broad
classification schemes that are designed to divide documents into broad
groups, such as those used by many information services to arrange
abstracts.

    The purposes of making the index term precise in relation to the
item are twofold: (1) to distinguish the item adequately from the rest of
the collection in order to reduce search time, and (2) to aid searchers
in determining if the document contains the information being sought.
The first purpose is relative to the collection, while the second is relative to the query; an essential conflict is that specificity realistically
must be relative to neither, but rather to the item. That is, it is extremely
unlikely that indexing the item more precisely than its subject warrants
will serve any useful purpose, and such a procedure would definitely
cause the part of the information content that was not included in the
indexing to be lost. On the other hand, indexing it less precisely in
effect loses information, causing the item to be lost among others on
the general subject and on other small parts of the general subject. Of

course, there is an important way in which the index terms should be designed to be of a precision relative to the needs of the collection and the queries to be expected. If the items as a whole are on broad subjects, but contain information on more precise subjects, then the system must provide for access to these narrow subjects as needed. However, this is less a matter of the specificity of the index terms than of the selection of idexable matter, discussed in Chapter 6. $Sp!$

In actual practice most systems attempt simply to identify items uniquely enough to keep search time below what is regarded as an acceptable maximum for the collection. No hard and fast rule can be set; at this level the issue is similar to the problem of how much information to include with the entry, discussed in Chapter 2. The point is to avoid requiring users to spend a great deal of time sorting out nonrelevant entries.

This discussion has involved primarily precoordinate systems; in a postcoordinate system coextensiveness is usually not achieved with single terms. The effect of coordination method on degree of coextensiveness is treated in Chapter 11.

Since in any given system providing greater coextensiveness will almost inevitably increase indexing and storage costs, the problem is to determine the extent to which such costs are justifiable as a means of saving cost to the user. Rules of thumb range from 3 to 15 undifferentiated entries, that is, those that are not distinguished from each other and thus require the searcher to access the original to determine which entries are useful. Such rules of thumb have value only within carefully stated limits, because the point of indexing is to minimize the time and effort expended between the original conception of a need and its satisfaction, not just the amount of time at a particular index location. When a user is looking at a group of entries, other factors such as the amount of information with the entry and ease of access to the originals affect the ease of moving from that stage to final satisfaction of the need. This relationship is further considered in Chapter 11.

Simple or Complex Structure

Index terms may vary in structure from single words or single items of notation to complex terms with modifiers or subsidiary notation. Subsidiary elements may extend to multiple levels and may be of several types. The individual terms of a postcoordinate vocabulary will ordinarily have a much simpler structure than those of a precoordinate one; the complexity may be introduced by the devices provided for postcoordination, whether simple Boolean logic or more complex devices such as roles, links, or weights.

Structure is not free; it is expensive to design into an index and expensive to maintain. Its sole purpose is to save user effort and cost by facilitating retrieval, both improving retrieval of relevant items and speeding discard of nonrelevant ones.

Unfortunately, structure can also be self-defeating, if it either is not self-evident or is so complex as to be difficult to keep in mind. Richmond (1959), approaching the matter from the point of view of concealed classification, showed how the complex vocabulary structure used in Library of Congress subject headings fails to serve users because it is not made explicit.

This subject heading system is a classic example of a complex structure in an alphabetical system. As it was originally designed, files under an access word could be broken down into many subarrangements, usually on the basis of punctuation. For example, the dash is used to show two kinds of subheadings: geographic, and all others; the comma is employed to make two kinds of inversions: national, and all others; parentheses set off identifying statements; natural language phases are also used. This is overlaid on the conceptual distinction between persons, places, and things. All this structure is hidden, however. There are no instructions for users who might therefore enter one subfile and fail to realize it was the wrong one. The difficulty is exacerbated by the card catalogue format, which makes it impossible to scan a large array of entries.

While the structure of the terms in this system remains essentially intact, use of the structure as an arranging device has essentially been abandoned. The structure probably was useful when users were aware of it, because files of many millions of items must be broken into manageable chunks somehow. It is regrettable that use of the structure in arrangement was abandoned rather than being revised and made explicit, since the bulk of the cost of producing it, in the form of maintenance and assignment of an extensive subject vocabulary, is still being incurred.

The findings of Raghavan and Iyer (1978) imply another limitation to both structural complexity and its use to increase coextensiveness. They made strings of subject terms and asked users to write phrases indicating the meaning of the strings. They found that if the phrases contained more than four components, the number of errors increased significantly.

The trend in recent years has been to use simple structures for terms, relying on postcoordination to narrow searches and provide precision. However, there is a tendency to impose some structure on such terms by the use of various devices such as roles, links, and weights. These are discussed in detail below. It is sufficient here to point out that the first two of these devices serve essentially the same purpose in a postcoordinate index as complex terms do in a precoordinate index with the added capability that it is easier to ignore them in searching the file, if desired.

The amount of structural complexity required is clearly a function of the size of the index. The more entries that are expected to accumulate under a given access word, the more differentiation should be provided. Since use of unaltered phrases introduces great problems of predictability in arrangement, and simply stringing substantives together can increase difficulty in determining the relationships of various words to each other, some structure must be introduced in order to permit differentiation while simultaneously simplifying search.

Citation Order in Complex Subject Terms

Usually if an index term is at all complex—that is, has a number of components—access to it by more than one of these components will be desirable. Furthermore, different queries will be satisfied by different arrangements of subsidiary elements. For example, a study of the interaction of temperature and water stress in plants which use Crassulacean Acid Metabolism (CAM) is of interest from a number of points of view other than the complete subject:

crassulacean acid metabolism
temperature stress
water stress
temperature stress in CAM plants
water stress in CAM plants
interaction of temperature and water stress
metabolism in plants
metabolism in plants under water stress conditions
metabolism in plants under temperature stress conditions
interaction of temperature and water stress on plant metabolism

Assuming a reasonably large file, with even this three-aspect document, once the access point is chosen there is a need for multiple subarrangements. To fill all the needs above requires the following sequence of aspects:

CAM plants, temperature stress, water stress
CAM plants, water stress
Water stress, temperature stress
Temperature stress
Metabolism in plants, temperature stress, water stress
Metabolism in plants, water stress

In a postcoordinate and/or computer-based system the matter can be taken care of more or less automatically; however, a precoordinate printed index is far less flexible, and the problem is one of considerable magnitude. A simple calculation will demonstrate this well enough. If there are n elements in an index term, the number of possible permutations of the elements is n!; thus a term containing 4 elements will permit 24 possible combinations of these elements; a term containing only 3 still has 6 possible combinations. Even assuming a human looked at all combinations and on the average only half were useful, we would still be left with 12 and 3 entries respectively.

Most printed indexes avoid the problem entirely by forbidding synonymous entries, requiring that each concept be entered in one place and one place only. In a closed index, that is, one whose final contents are known, some judicious duplication may be used, but all duplication increases the size of the index. It can have unanticipated consequences in an open index, leading to far larger files than planned, and/or to inconsistency when indexers fail to provide for the duplications.

If a particular combination will occur frequently, it is easiest to select only one form, and to make "see" reference(s) from the unused forms to the used forms of the combination. This still leaves us with the vast majority of combinations that do not occur often enough to be worth the extra step of a cross-reference. There have been a number of strategies, none entirely successful, for dealing with these. (Better strategies might have been developed by now if the availability of Boolean logic and postcoordinate search had not made it appear likely that the problem would soon vanish. If this is the case it is unfortunate, because the vast majority of indexes, and the vast majority of index uses, are still in the form of human lookup on printed pages.)

These strategies may be divided into two categories of rules and procedures: (1) those designed to make the order of elements predictable, thereby reducing the need for permutation; and (2) those designed simply to reduce the number of elements to be permuted.

Predictability of the Order of Elements

Chain indexing is the best-known of the procedures that take this approach to providing access to the elements of a complex term. Chain procedure normally (but not always) requires that information first be assigned a classification notation; a "chain" of terms that in effect reverses the order of elements in the classification is then devised, and entries are made by successively dropping the first term from the beginning of the chain. Chain indexing is more complex than this simple explanation indicates, but this is the fundamental process.

Chain procedure guarantees that the same order of elements will be followed for different terms, but it cannot prevent the same subsidiary element from being entered in different places, depending on the citation order of the classification array used as the source for index terms. For instance, if the citation order of the elements in the preceding example is:

Metabolism in plants
Crassulacean Acid Metabolism (CAM)
Temperature stress
Water stress,

then the following entries would be generated:

Water stress: temperature stress: CAM plants
Temperature stress: CAM plants
CAM plants
Metabolism in plants

This sequence loses the subjects of water stress in CAM plants, and of either kind of stress in plant metabolism in general. Of course, in a typical faceted system, temperature stress and water stress would be assigned to the same facet, requiring two index strings instead of the first two entries above:

water stress: CAM plants
temperature stress: CAM plants

This array loses the interaction of the two types of stress.

Because the order achieved in chain procedure is determined by the facets that are present, term pairs may be separated, as in the following:

Textiles: Dyeing: C.T. Acid Blue 25: Effluents: Recovery: Adsorption: Carbon, Activated: Mass Transfer
Textiles: Dyeing: Effluents: Recovery: Adsorption: Wood

The above two entries on effluent recovery were separated by five entries on other aspects of textile dyeing in the 1980 *British Technology Index*.

Nonetheless, compared with the procedures it was intended to replace, where the extra entries simply were not made, chain procedure was a considerable improvement. However, it was soon clear that human intervention was required to add entries and to prevent useless ones from consuming index space; it was a logical next step to move away from classification entirely by devising an independent indexing system whose term elements may be cycled in a predictable and useful way.

PRECIS is this outgrowth. In this system, indexers follow a series of specific syntactic rules in developing the component parts of an index term that can then be manipulated automatically by rule to produce useful index entries. The number of entries produced is also under the control of the indexer, and can therefore be varied to suit the needs of a particular system.

These are the most prominent examples of systems of rules and procedures designed to reduce—while keeping their location predictable—the number of entries generated for a particular complex index term.

Reducing the Number of Elements to be Permuted

These procedures as a group are less systematic than the preceding ones, concentrating on finding words or terms for which access points need not be generated rather than on limiting the number of entries required by making the order of elements predictable. Examples are the rules of the *Permuterm Subject Index*, in which certain words are automatically precoordinated, and SLIC (Selective Listing in Context) (Sharp, 1966) indexes, which coordinate each element with every other element, but in a fixed rather than permuted order, causing each term to generate $2^{n-1} - 1$ entries instead of $n!$ entries, where n is the number of elements. Thus a term of four components A, B, C, and D will generate 7 entries instead of 24.

ABCD
ACD
AD
BCD
BD
CD
D

The difficulty with all such systems is that unlike the more complex procedures described above, they generate entries based on the co-occurrence of words, usually in titles. There is no guarantee that such co-occurrence implies a relationship, and therefore the entry produced may be useless. However, these methods do generate additional entries quickly and cheaply, and will usually produce a high proportion of useful ones.

Structure in Postcoordinate Indexes

A major problem in postcoordinate indexing is the need to show relations between terms in order to avoid erroneous retrieval on the basis of index terms that simply happen to be assigned to the same document, but are not related to each other within that document—the "false drop" problem. The primary tools used for this purpose are roles and links: roles to show the way in which a term is used in a given document (e.g., thing versus part of a larger thing), and links to show that two terms are actually used in conjunction with each other in the document. These are directly analogous to such devices as modifiers and subheadings in precoordinate indexes, as Artandi and Hines (1963) have shown.

These devices do add complexity to the indexing and searching processes, so it is well to consider whether their value is worth their cost. There are two studies that more or less confirm that the answer is negative. Blagden (1966) found that about 30% of the noise (false drops) in a system which split terms to a high degree (thereby presumably increasing recall but also increasing retrieval of irrelevant documents) could have been avoided by use of roles (11%) or links (19%). Over half the noise, however, was due to "bad vocabulary choice" (not further defined, but not indexing errors since these are separately allocated). Thirty percent of the noise is not an insignificant amount, but it seems likely that resources would be better spent dealing first with the larger source of error, the vocabulary, particularly since the unusually high degree of term splitting in the system testing would give roles and links a larger part in the attainment of precision than in more typical systems.

Meanwhile, Montague (1965) found that in a system covering chemical patents, indexed at an average depth of 40 terms each, links had no effect on recall and precision, but accounted for 4% of total indexing cost. Roles accounted for 11% of indexing cost. While they increased precision, errors in their application also reduced recall.

These results are hardly definitive, but perhaps more telling is the fact that newly developed systems do not seem to be including roles and links today; they may not be dropped from ongoing systems very often, but few systems are started up with them. Blagden (1968) summarized the literature on these devices, finding it inconclusive. It is noteworthy, however, that of the work he reviews, several reports came out against roles and links, with only one favoring their use.

✗

Relationships

Two of the three factors discussed in this chapter are closely related, while the third is less so, but may be a factor in some circumstances. It is almost unavoidable that as index terms become more coextensive with items of information, their structure must become more complex. The index term will have more components, and as noted above in the discussion of structural complexity, simply stringing words together in an unstructured fashion results in ambiguity.

Introduction of structure generally results in deviation from strict natural language, either to classification notation, or to modifications of word order, accompanied by the development of specialized syntactical elements.

Thus, it may be best to view the decision about coextensiveness as the primary one. If terms are to be reasonably coextensive with items, then terms must become more complex and highly structured; furthermore, the introduction of structure tends to lead to at least some degree of artificiality, or classification, in the language. The reverse, however, is not true; index items may be highly structured and/or the language may be constructed without the terms being coextensive with the items of information.

Summary

The most important overall choices in design of terminology of an indexing system have been covered here. They include the choice between natural and constructed languages; degree of coextensiveness of the terms with the subject of the item, and complexity of term structure. Pure natural language is rarely used except in simple-term systems; addition of more complex terms almost inevitably results in development of a specialized grammar and syntax. The more complex the grammar and syntax, the more complex the structure of the terms. Larger indexes require a greater degree of coextensiveness of terms in order to reduce search time to a minimum by differentiating information items from each other. All these are interrelated, particularly as the index grows, requiring more structure and coextensiveness to differentiate the larger number of items. Furthermore, use of complex terms raises issues of citation order, as it is neither possible nor useful to make entries under all possible permutations of such terms. The designer of a postcoordinate index has related choices to make in the use of roles and links.

As terms become more coextensive, they generally also must become more complex and structure will be introduced. Furthermore, use of structure will tend to result in deviation from strict natural language.

The American National Standards Institute (1974) and the British Standards Institution (1979) have published standards that provide guidance on some of the decisions in this and the next chapter, particularly on choice and form of terms and on thesaural relationships. Keen (1977) has provided descriptive information on these factors also.

Terminology Authority Design

Introduction

The choices to be made in the design and structure of the terms in a system based on assignment indexing were discussed in Chapter 9; this chapter discusses the choices to be made in the design of the vocabulary authority tool itself. There are five major variables:

1. literary warrant or structure of knowledge as the criterion for admission of terms,
2. enumeration or synthesis, or some combination of the two,
3. the extent to which the authority is prescriptive or permissive regarding use of terms not actually present in it,
4. size of the vocabulary, and
5. whether to provide syndetics, and if so, their type and structure.

The first four of these choices are discussed in this chapter; matters of syndetic structure have been covered in Chapter 5 as an issue of file design.

The goals are to provide terms that:

1. permit adequate differentiation of the material to be indexed,
2. make this differentiation with the minimum number of different terms,
3. are easily intelligible to users and indexers, and
4. describe accurately the topics to be indexed.

Literary Warrant or Structure of Knowledge

This question has two aspects, one of policy in initial design of the vocabulary, and another that arises on an ongoing basis.

Policy in Initial Design

Shall the permitted terms be derived by analysis of the subjects that occur in the body of knowledge to be covered by the index, or from those that are found to occur with significant frequency in the literature to be indexed, or from some combination of the two?

While there will obviously be a great deal of overlap between the terminology of the subject and that of its literature, the coincidence will be far from complete. Terms derived from the subject will cover the area of interest completely and fairly uniformly, but the areas of special interest—and therefore of heavy emphasis in the literature—will not be nearly as uniform. The development of a subject at any one time will be far from even, and the shorter the time span covered by the index the more significant this unevenness will be. However, the fact that uniformity of coverage will increase with time is really not of much help; the span of time to consider will be very long—decades or more—and it is not possible to predict future areas of interest from past ones.

Devising a vocabulary solely on the basis of indexing leads to an authority based on the literature, containing only terms that have been found actually to be used there. Thus the criterion of literary warrant that has been generally accepted since Hulme (1911) stated it early in this century will be satisfied. However, if the development of the vocabulary is limited solely to terms as they are found to be required by the literature indexed, the terms will be inconsistently formulated, meaning that the placement of topics will not be predictable. Perhaps worse, a coherent reference structure will be lacking, so that indexers and users will not be led from their points of entry into the vocabulary to the appropriate terms. This happens because a purely ad hoc approach does not lead to good opportunities for looking at the entire structure and developing the needed relationships.

On the other hand, developing the vocabulary by deciding which area is to be covered, and then gleaning terms from various sources and from subect experts' suggestions may produce a logical, coherent vocabulary that covers and explicates the area of knowledge very well, but bears only a moderate resemblance to the subject coverage of the literature that is actually being indexed. This happens because not all parts of a field are of equal interest at any one time. Lancaster (1972) presents a useful summary of the problems with both approaches.

Thus, reliance on the use of actual indexing without overall co-ordination in development of the authority will produce a vocabulary that matches the literature, but that is inconsistent and offers little guidance to the individual who enters system from other than the approved point. On the other hand, complete reliance on selection of terms from glossaries, by experts, or by means of other devices not based on actual work with the literature can produce a vocabulary that is well thought out, coherent, and provides ample guidance to users, but that lacks needed terms, and is heavily bulked up with terms that do not reflect the literature covered.

A mix of methods is clearly indicated. Findings from either actual indexing or analysis of documents that would be covered by the index should be relied on almost exclusively for selection of concepts to be included in the vocabulary; then other resources—including analysis of the developing vocabulary itself—may be used for guidance in selection of the form of terms, or of one of several possible ways of expressing a concept.

Analysis of the vocabulary and access to subject experts, whether directly or at second hand, are extremely important in development of the syndetic structure; the latter should be used judiciously here too, because while the relations among concepts and the relations among needs for literature indexed under terms will overlap, they will by no means coincide totally. Any system that makes broader, narrower, and related term references or their equivalents on the basis of the relations among the concepts rather than the items indexed will inevitably make many references among terms where the material is unlikely to be of interest for the same or similar queries. At the same time it will fail to draw together less-related concepts where documents of related interest are entered. For instance, in the Library of Congress Subject Headings, the concepts represented by the terms "Diplomatic negotiations in international disputes" and "Iran—Foreign relations—US" are not so closely related as to require cross references, but in the context of the Iranian hostage crisis in 1979–1981, any index using this system would certainly enter closely related documents under these two headings.

However, a policy of adding terms and making references solely on the basis of literary warrant prevents the system from anticipating future needs, a limitation that is particularly important in early stages of development. During start-up it may be useful, on a carefully limited basis, to integrate terms that are known to be needed for concepts in the literature, even if they have not yet been required for indexing. Later, however, it is reasonable to take the position that if a term has not been required in a year or two of indexing, there is no sound reason, aside from an actual document on the subject, to assume it will ever be needed. Obviously, new subjects arise all the time and must be incorporated, but it is part of their novelty that they cannot reasonably be anticipated. For every new term added in anticipation of need that turned out to be warranted within a reasonable time, several more useless ones would probably also be included.

Ongoing Indexing

The issue to be considered here has already been touched on above. The literature must be primary in selection of the topics to be included in the vocabulary, but it is dominant in selection of the terminology only to the extent to which the vocabulary of the anticipated users and that of the authors overlap. While the overlap will be high, it will not be perfect, and the question needs to be considered explicitly. Soergel (1974, pp. 66–67) concisely points out that there is no such thing as "the" user or for that matter "the" author; that there will be variation in users' and authors' vocabularies and that, furthermore, a given user may need a document for a purpose different from the one the author had in mind in writing it. Therefore, consideration of all vocabularies to be expected in the index is essential.

Enumeration or Synthesis of Terms

This choice applies only to systems that permit the use of complex terms—terms that may embrace more than one concept. A system that permits only terms denoting simple concepts will not allow for synthesis. In an enumerative system all possible complexities of subjects to be brought out in indexing are explicitly provided for in the vocabulary authority; a synthetic system provides rules for combining simple terms to cover the complex concepts.

A purely enumerative system would attempt to provide explicitly for all of the conjunctions and modifications of terms to be allowed in the system. A purely synthetic system would provide what amounted to a set of building blocks, or fundamental terms, together with rules for combining these into the complex concepts required for the system.

Many thesauri today are purely enumerative, but they tend to be limited to relatively simple terms; they are designed to permit, in machine search at least, the equivalent of synthesis at output. I know of no indexing system using complex terms that is completely enumerative. Probably the closest one is the Library of Congress Classification, which has no general provisions for synthesis, and instead provides for division of certain subjects according to specialized tables.

The ultimate in synthesis was surely the early versions of Ranganathan's Colon Classification, but in later editions he found it necessary to enumerate more subjects as the limitations of synthesis became more evident. The fundamental limitation is probably the human mind. The user who enters the system must break down the question into the same simpler components as the designers of the system have provided in order to be able to locate the answer. If there is no general acceptance or immediate intuition of what the components of a complex concept are, it is probably not feasible to build it up by synthesis. The classic question (now obsolete) regarding synthesis in the Colon Classification had to do with the "personality" of a typewriter. True, the concept may be expressed as a machine that is used to mechanize the process of putting characters on paper, but to do so somehow loses the essence of what a typewriter is all about.

In an enumerative system the only task of the user, whether the indexer or the searcher, is to find the way in which a concept may be expressed in the system. Counteracting this ease of use, however, is the bulkiness and rigidity produced by the attempt to list each and every concept. Much repetition will be found, since many elements of concepts occur in much the same pattern of conjunction with many other concepts. For example, all kinds of crops may be bred, planted, tended, harvested, processed, distributed, and prepared. To enumerate all this for every crop is really pointless.

At the same time, the enumerative system lacks the facility of providing for some unanticipated subjects that judicious synthesis can permit. To continue the example above, if any crop may be synthesized with any operation on a crop, then if a previously underexploited crop becomes a center of breeding interest, the index term for it is automatically available, even though it never existed before. To take the example a bit further, if a totally new crop is developed, the provision for its aspects is already present; the crop itself must be integrated into the system, but that is all.

However, if extensive synthesis is used, all users have a great deal to master; not just the terms in the system that will, it is true, be fewer than in an enumerative system, but also the rules for synthesizing them. If the system permits extensive synthesis, the task of learning can become very involved. It will be necessary to learn which facets may be attached to each other and in what order.

One pitfall that should be avoided, however, is requiring users to break down what will to them be unitary concepts (usually detectable linguistically) in order to re-synthesize them. For instance, the breakdown of "Bibliography" into "Books—description" in Kaiser's (1911; 1926) concrete–process system is a disservice. It requires users to make the separation and later reunification for the sole purpose of fitting an arbitrary system design. The designer should never lose sight of the fact that by far the most important—if not the only—criterion of value for an indexing system is its usability. Many elements such as cost and ease of updating enter into usability, but theoretical nicety is not always one of them.

Therefore, as with so many other choices, the designer must attempt to find the balance of enumeration and synthesis that works best for a particular system. Nearly all subject areas have some facets that are applicable more or less across the board, and others that must be provided for individually. The former are readily synthesizable, while the latter will best be enumerated.

In synthesis, room must be made for all aspects at every point where they could be added, even if only a few are likely to be used at any one point. An enumerative scheme need provide only for those that are actually used—though if another comes into use with a given subject, the enumerative scheme will have to be expanded, possibly at some inconvenience, to provide for it.

Another advantage of enumeration over synthesis is that if a notation is used it can be more compact. The enumerative notation need not provide space to synthesize many facets when only a few are likely to be needed at any one point. An extreme case of this may be seen in the Dewey Docimal Classification, in which extensive synthetic capabilities have been grafted onto a scheme that in its original design was basically enumerative, providing synthesis for only a few facets. Use of the present synthetic features leads to extremely long notation because of the devices required to distinguish facets from one another within the limitations of the 10 numeric characters used for the notation. An available option, of course, is the use of special symbols, such as punctuation marks, to indicate each facet, but decoding these imposes yet another burden on users. Issues of notation design are considered in Chapter 4: here it is sufficient to point out that, if users are expected to make use of the information contained in the notation, it is essential that it be decoded for them, in which case its complexity will not be a great barrier.

Use of facet analysis techniques, well described by Vickery (1960), can greatly simplify the task of achieving a reasonable balance between enumeration and synthesis in a given system. Study of the concepts in the system will normally show that they fall into definable categories such as things, their parts, operations, places, and periods of time. While this list may readily be seen to be a rather free adaptation of Ranganathan's Personality, Matter, Energy, Space, and Time, these are examples only. They may not be especially useful without alteration for a given subject, and others may be required. For instance, facet analysis in architecture would lead to recognition of such facets as type (purpose) of building, style, mode of ornamentation, period, and place; furthermore, other aspects such as the larger complex of which a building is a part might be germane. The facets to be used in a given system should not be rigidly set in advance. It is essential to study the universe to be included in the system and the anticipated user needs to set up facets. Once this has been done, however, a balance between enumeration and synthesis is more readily achieved.

Prescriptive versus Permissive

Every system will fall somewhere along a continuum in the extent of its acceptance of use of terms that are not actually present in the vocabulary authority. In a highly prescriptive authority, only terms that are actually present in the vocabulary may be used in indexing; a permissive authority grants more leeway. It may be regarded as a list of terms for which permission for use has already been granted, leaving the question of use of other terms open, rather than one that prohibits use of most or all nonlisted terms. There are two aspects to the decision on degree of prescriptiveness or permissiveness: (1) the freedom with which new terms may be added to the authority and (2) the extent to which terms not in the authority, and not candidates for addition, may be used.

The choice between enumeration and synthesis may seem at first glance to be a special case of this continuum, but the issue considered here is a different one. The selection of enumeration or synthesis indicates a decision as to whether the vocabulary should contain unitary terms or "building blocks" that may be combined in more or less rigorously specified ways. An enumerative or synthetic vocabulary may be either prescriptive or permissive; the one choice is of the way terms are built up; the other is whether the indexer may go outside the formal vocabulary for terms.

Freedom to Add New Terms

No vocabulary can be completely frozen and still remain useful for indexing. Topics of interest change and unanticipated ones arise. While some of these may be fitted under existing terms without doing too much violence to their meaning, if this practice is carried on for long, items will be indexed by terms that are not really appropriate and diverse subjects will be mixed under the same term, reducing the value of both vocabulary and index.

On the other hand, adding new terms to a vocabulary is an expensive matter. It is necessary to verify that the scope of the term is really well defined and that there is no undue overlap with existing terms; then the new term must be integrated into the syndetic structure. Once a term has been accepted into the vocabulary it must be maintained until it is deleted, something that should happen as rarely as possible because it raises the problem of what to do with the documents that have been indexed under the deleted term.

Many concepts appear only once or very rarely; others may enjoy a brief vogue, only to vanish from the literature. The principle of specific entry would call for entry of a unique concept under its name, but this is not of a great deal of help here, since no index is ever completely specific with regard to all topics. The designer must therefore consider what limits to place on specificity in a given situation. The best criterion generally is probably the amount of material that will appear, not under the rare term, but under the general term where it would be incorporated. If there is so much material under the general term that the reader will have difficulty in sorting out the unique term(s), the material should probably be entered under the rare term. Another obvious criterion is the amount of interest to be expected in the subject, but presumably the item would not be indexed at all unless some interest were expected; the degree is virtually impossible to predict with any assurance, since needs change.

The rarely occurring concept is a good candidate for nonspecific entry, saving the burden of maintaining an index term for a very small payoff. The subject that enjoys a brief vogue is not as easily dismissed, however. If it is at all distinctive, it is likely to be of interest later, at least in the historical sense, and therefore should not be incorporated in with more general material. However, to go on maintaining the term in the vocabulary authority indefinitely is costly. Two options are available: (1) to use a facility for indexing with terms not in the vocabulary (discussed in the following section); or (2) to maintain for searchers a record of terms deleted from the vocabulary, together with the period in which they were used. Since re-indexing is rarely feasible, maintenance of such a record prevents these documents from effectively being lost in the system.

Use of Terms not in the Official Vocabulary

Only a system that consists of pigeonholes, whether enumerative or synthetic, can function effectively without providing for use of terms not present in the vocabulary authority and not intended to be added. There are simply so many specific entities—people, places, organisms, etc.—that it is neither feasible nor desirable to include them in the authority. In addition there are the rare or briefly in vogue terms mentioned above.

It is common for a system to have policies permitting entry of specific entities, either under defined rules, or using some other authority. For instance, the Library of Congress Subject Headings implicitly include all names of individuals, personal or corporate, by means of the policy that provides for entry of such entities according to the *Anglo-American Cataloguing Rules*.

Another type of practice is the use of "identifiers," as they are called in systems such as ERIC and others. Identifiers look like thesaurus terms, but typically are neither controlled not integrated into the syndetic structure. Such terms will be inconsistent in both use and form unless a record is maintained. Even then the failure to provide cross-references prevents users from being led to these specifics from more general terms. Of course, if entry is faithfully duplicated under the most appropriate authorized term, with the identifier simply providing extra access, this objection is eliminated.

Typically, the types of terms maintained in the controlled vocabulary are different from those permitted as identifiers, or implicitly included on the basis of some other authority. Conceptual subject terms, general or specialized, will be fully controlled, while jargon and vogue words and names of specific entities will be relegated to the lesser-control category.

Unless a pigeonhole approach is intended, some sort of provision for these terms is essential. They cannot simply be omitted from the vocabulary, but they cannot all be given full syndetic structure either. Most fruitful will probably be a combination of approaches. It seems wisest to duplicate entries for specific entities and jargon or vogue terms under the specific term and the authorized vocabulary term wherever feasible. If this is done there is no need to integrate the vogue terms into the vocabulary, though in all cases a record is needed to maintain consistency. If double entry is not feasible, then provision can be designed into the system for temporary references leading from the vocabulary terms to the vogue ones. Such references would still be much less costly than full integration into the syndetic apparatus. In any case it is very important to permit use of the vogue terms because these are likely to be the ones where people will search first.

Size of the Vocabulary

In a way the decision on the size of the vocabulary—the number of terms it may contain—is really determined by the outcome of a number of other decisions (see Chapter 11), but it is also worth looking at briefly as a factor by itself. The possible range is from the descriptor systems of Mooers, designed so that all the terms can fit on the one side of a large sheet of paper, to the Library of Congress Subject Headings, or if the chemical terms are taken into account, the authority for the indexes to *Chemical Abstracts*. The range can be from a few hundred to several tens of thousands of terms, depending on size and purpose of the system.

The fundamental purpose of an index system is to speed the finding of items of information that fill a need; this purpose may also be conceived negatively as aiding the rejection of items that do not fill a given need. To fulfill this purpose, however stated, requires that the system have available enough terms adequately to differentiate the items from each other. The ratio of vocabulary size to collection size required to reach this goal depends on kinds of items and kinds of requests, and the number of terms typically assigned to each item. If documents and/ or requests are on highly precise, narrow topics, more terms will be required for adequate differentiation than if the opposite is true. Furthermore, the larger the number of terms assigned to each item, the more terms are required to avoid having too many items posted to each term.

Relationships among the Factors

Regardless of whether a system most strongly emphasizes literary warrant or the structure of knowledge in development of the vocabulary, it must have some flexibility in adding new terms if it is to remain current. If knowledge were stable, indexing would eventually become unnecessary because all would be known. However, systems based on the structure of knowledge are likely to be less permissive, because the principle of literary warrant explicitly requires addition of new terms as they are warranted. A system based in literary warrant is for the same reason likely to be freer about accepting terms whose use is expected to be limited.

An enumerative vocabulary must be larger than a synthetic one since it uses distinct terms to label many concepts that are accommodated by synthesis of two or more terms, each of which may appear in a variety of other combinations in a synthetic system. An enumerative system is also likely to be more permissive than a synthetic one, since the latter frequently has the option of achieving specificity by synthesis of existing terms instead of adding new ones.

A more permissive vocabulary will be larger in terms of the number of different terms actually used in indexing; the formal vocabulary may, however, be smaller than a more prescriptive one because large groups of terms may be included by example or instruction without listing each member of the group explicitly in the vocabulary.

Summary

In this chapter were discussed the implications of some decisions for the design of the terminology authority as a whole. A balance between development of the vocabulary from actual indexing and abstract selection of terms on the basis of their importance to the subject must be achieved in order to have a system that reflects the literature but is also consistent and has a useful syndetic structure. The system based on literary warrant is likely to be more permissive because of its explicit recognition that terms encountered in the literature are valid for indexing use.

While both enumerative and synthetic elements are present in nearly all systems, a balance is necessary between the size demanded by enumeration and the requirement that users learn not only terms but also rules for combining them in a synthetic system. Synthesis has become more prominent as system designers have recognized that all knowledge cannot be enumerated. Facet analytic techniques, flexibly applied, are of great value in designing systems for the optimum amount of synthesis.

A system should be somewhat permissive in accepting terms not in the formal vocabulary, but careful provision must be made to ensure that documents are not lost to the searcher who relies on the subject vocabulary for terms. Duplicate entry under the formal vocabulary terms is the most desirable way around this barrier. There are many groups of terms, particularly names of specific entities, that are needed for indexing, but that would greatly enlarge the vocabulary if they were explicitly included. Also, jargon words and those that occur only rarely need to be available for use.

The size of the vocabulary may vary widely, depending on the size of the system and the kinds of needs it is intended to serve. Size is also affected by choices between permissiveness and prescriptiveness and between enumeration and synthesis, with enumerative and formal prescriptive vocabularies being larger, but permissive indexes containing more different terms.

P A R T   V

Summary

Relationships among the Major Choices

The preceding chapters of this work have each treated the choices to be made in one or a few closely related areas in index system design. This chapter takes a broader point of view, examining the ways in which the choices in one broad area constrain those in another. This arrangement of the material is based on the logic of the organization of this book and does not reflect the relative importance of the topics treated. That is, this chapter brings out relationships that cross over the boundaries of the major areas in the rest of the book, but the topics treated here should not be seen as any more or less important than those treated in earlier chapters.

Relationships among the choices in each major section of the work are treated first, followed by those that cut across these large areas. Since the aspects explored in Part II are so diverse, the interplay of the variables in this part is more important than in other parts, and therefore receives more extensive treatment.

The chapter closes with a case study of the application of all the alternatives in the design of an actual index.

The File

The number of entries per document, the number of documents, and the total size of the file are very closely interrelated. Given a particular type of index term and a set amount of information with each entry, the total size of the file is almost a simple multiple of the number of entries per document and the number of documents. Typically, the approximate desired maximum size of the file may be taken as the constraint, and up to that size one trades off between more or fewer entries and fewer or more documents, depending on the perceived needs. Therefore these factors tend to influence other decisions much as though they were a single factor, and they are so treated in this chapter.

The storage medium strongly influences both the amount of information that can be carried with each entry and the number of entries likely to be provided. The more space-consuming the physical file, the tighter the constraints on the amount of information and the number of access points.

Print and microform are conceptually but not actually equivalent here. The latter is essentially just a physical miniaturization of the former, and microform indexes generally are different from print indexes only in that their sheer size would most likely have prevented them from being published at all in hard copy. That is, microform indexes do not appear to be published in this form simply to save money, but rather to make possible the production of the information in any form at all. Thus, indexes are not typically published in microform instead of print in order to make it feasible to provide more access points, or to be able to provide more information with each entry—though this would certainly be possible. If this were the case we would see the equivalent of a *Chemical Abstracts* index on microform with abstracts carried with each entry, or a microform *Resources in Education* with access from both major and minor descriptors for the items.

While there is no evidence to support any conclusions, it seems reasonable to conjecture that microform is perceived as so difficult to use that it is worthwhile only if there is no other option; that if the choice is between more access points or more information in microform and fewer or less of these in print the greater ease of using print is perceived as compensating for the inferior access. The truth may simply be that user resistance to microform is considered to be great enough that no one is willing to risk its use if any other option is available.

Card-form storage is a variant of the printed form, which can have a dramatic impact on the amount of information carried with the entry, as well as a lesser impact on the number of entries allowed for each document. If an entire card is allocated to each entry, then any information up to the maximum the card can hold will have no impact on the physical size of the index; hence there is a tendency in such indexes to give a great deal of information with each entry. The significance of this is clearly shown by comparison of card- and book-form library catalogues. For the same reason, addition of each new entry to a card-form index increases the size of the index to a greater degree than in the printed page mode, so the number of entries is likely to be kept smaller in the former.

It is in the use of machine storage that the impact of the storage medium on the various factors in size becomes very evident. It is common for indexes to be available in both machine-readable form and print or microform; almost invariably the machine-readable form offers a great many more access points with, as far as the user is concerned, complete information with each entry. This is feasible because each additional entry for a document in computer storage requires storage only of the added index term information, even though far more information about the document may be retrieved in a way that makes it appear to users almost as though all the information were stored with each entry. Since for the foreseeable future machine access will be more costly than manual access, the two means of storage are best seen as complementary, not competitive.

The mode of searching the index, whether precoordinate or post-coordinate, will also affect its size, though the precise effect may be influenced by other factors as well. Almost automatically, postcoordinate search means that concepts that might be expressed in a single complex term in a precoordinate index will be decomposed into smaller elements. This effectively increases the number of access points and the space required for locators. Whether it actually increases the physical size of the index depends on decisions made about the amount of information provided with each entry. Precoordinate indexes commonly carry enough information at every entry point to permit identification of the document, whereas postcoordinate indexes may carry only a simple accession number or other locating device. This may even represent a difference in number of lookup stages, since the accession number in the postcoordinate index often leads only to a bibliographic listing, which then gives the information required to locate the document.

A number of different factors influence or are influenced by the mode of search and the storage medium. While these two factors are technically separable, they are most usefully treated together. (Computer storage solely for the purpose of producing a print or microform product is not considered in this work.)

If computer storage and search are to be used, it is practical to design the system so that more information is carried with the entry as the user sees it. That is, while typically only a pointer is physically part of the index entry in present-day computer storage technologies, access to the information pointed to is so fast that to the user it appears that all the document information is available with the entry. At the same time, the computer system can permit the user to specify the amount of information to appear with each entry, up to the total that is actually available within the system. The user can therefore elect to see only a little of the information if the need is to screen a great many entries rapidly; if a careful selection is to be made, the full information can be listed for each entry. The logical conclusion of this is the making available of full text at each access point. As more full text becomes available, usually as a by-product of computer typesetting, and as the cost of storage decreases, more full-text databases are being developed.

The type of arrangement used is strongly influenced by the choice between human and computer search of the file. Rather, what may be conceived as the results of the act of arrangement—the human-readable array of entries next to each other—is affected. The physical arrangement on a machine-readable medium may or may not be affected. Normally for indexes maintained in an eye-readable medium, space constraints force a selection of one or a few types of array; with computer search many more types are possible, including, in addition to the normal ones found in printed indexes, listings showing which words fall next to each other and listings sorted on word endings instead of word beginnings. Other factors that can be used to achieve the desired array include a wide variety of nonsubject characteristics such as language or intellectual level—in fact anything that has been found worthwhile to add to the record.

The type of syndetic structure, if any, to provide, how to develop it, and whether or not to integrate it within the main file are all influenced by the mode of search to be used. In computer search the syndetic structure can, instead of suggesting that the user try other access point(s), cause retrieval of the items located at these other points. This may be done automatically without even informing the user (converting OPEC to Organization of Petroleum Exporting Countries or vice versa, for example), or the user may be informed of the expansion which led to the retrieval, as would be desirable when the retrieval is on the basis of a related or narrower term. The user may, as in the MEDLARS tree structures, be permitted to specify whether automatic retrieval on the basis of the syndetic structure is desired.

This form of aid, however, requires a much more rigorously developed structure than the rather casual relationships specified in most printed indexes. If the capabilities of machine search are to be truly exploited in amplification of the syndetic structure, it is vital to expend significant resources on developing a structure that can support this use. While a conventional thesaurus structure is of great value, attention must also be given to connections warranted by the literature and by subjects of search, even if not warranted by the formal meanings of terms.

There is nothing about the mode of search to reduce the need for a syndetic structure, but the arguments relating to its inclusion in the body of the index are different. I know of no machine-based systems today that actually retrieve references to other terms in a formal syndetic structure in response to a search query for the documents indexed by a term. If these references are accessible at all, they are retrieved by searching a separate file. It is easier to call up a different file from a terminal than it is to search out a separate volume on a shelf to retrieve the syndetic structure, but this mode still imposes a barrier on the searcher. The option could certainly be provided to retrieve the syndetic structure with the document references if desired. One reason for not doing so is economic; if the system would in any case only present the list of references, requiring the user to key in the desired ones, it is probably more conservative of search time to keep a printed thesaurus next to the terminal in the expectation that the formal syndetic structure can be followed up before search is begun.

This limitation does reduce flexibility when the conception of the search changes while it is in progress, and the art of presenting menus to users, whether alone or in combination with other information, is well enough developed to permit the presentation of the cross-references for retrieval, meaning that integration of the references will be more economic of user time.

Unless the file is to be computer stored, there is little opportunity for automatic development of the syndetic structure. Similarly, the concept of the extensive entry vocabulary, guiding the user more or less automatically from the entry point to the point(s) at which the desired information is actually stored, is essentially impractical to implement outside the computer because it will consume too much space.

On the other hand, the penalty to the user of dropping some kinds of syndetics is different, and probably smaller, in a machine-searchable index. With such capabilities as truncation of terms or calling up a selection of retrieved documents to examine other terms used in indexing them, the user, with some effort, gets an approximation of a syndetic structure even if no formal one is present. A poor approximation, relying on alphabetical proximity in most circumstances, but an approximation.

The AID (Associative Interactive Dictionary) system (Doszkocs, 1978) at the National Library of Medicine may presage the future, as it permits users to have the benefits of both formal syndetics and automatically developed term associations. A searcher invoking the AID system is presented with a list of terms ranked according to their degree of association with the search terms. The association measures are derived by measuring co-occurrence with the search terms in the collection.

It has often been claimed that an advantage of a classified over an alphabetical array is that much less is required in the way of a syndetic structure, since the classified array brings related topics together. While the claim is true in some ways, it is also oversimplified.

A classified array brings out some relationships, but unavoidably only those selected as grouping criteria in the classification design. Other relationships are distributed throughout the classification. Therefore, the location of all topics in the classification cannot be self-evident. To be useful, a classification of any size requires a syndetic structure in the form of an alphabetical index to aid the user who wants a specific topic, but does not know where it has been placed. The equivalent of cross-references is also required to send the user from alternative locations for a concept to the one where it has been placed.

Conceptually, a sound syndetic structure in an alphabetical index provides a kind of classified approach to a tool that is essentially alphabetical, while the alphabetical index to a classification provides a kind of alphabetical approach to a tool which is essentially classified. An example is the Thesaurofacet system (Aitchison, 1970) in which an alphabetical and a classified arrangement are combined (though produced in two files), neither one being subordinated to the other. A full syndetic structure is provided, but it is dispersed between the alphabetical and the classified files.

The Vocabulary

A very obvious relationship is that between the degree of coextensiveness of terms and the size of the categories into which concepts are divided, that is, the relative breadth of the terms. The more coextensive the terms, the smaller the categories will necessarily be.

Likewise, the more coextensive the terms, the more permissive the vocabulary must normally be. True, with a highly synthetic system whose elements are also reasonably precise, a great many very narrow unanticipated concepts can be accommodated, but it is inherently impossible to include everything in this way, and very ineffective to try.

Therefore considerable permissiveness is likely to be required. Conversely, a pigeonhole-type system will normally be prescriptive, because the pigeonholes will have been set up in advance. It is difficult to develop a permissive system based on a classification notation because such notations really must be developed in advance and all at once.

Almost by definition, a system that attempts to provide relatively coextensive terms must be based on literary warrant, since the terms are based directly on the documents. Of course, the structure of knowledge may be the primary influence in development of the vocabulary, but the provision of coextensiveness will immediately require heavy reliance on the literature. A high degree of coextensiveness also implies synthesis, since the required number of coextensive terms can hardly be enumerated. For one thing, they cannot be anticipated in advance. Synthetic systems usually contain more complex terms than enumerative ones, simply because the synthesis allows for and even encourages the complexity, while the necessity of enumeration discourages complexity. The rules for synthesis will also obviously affect citation order in complex terms; in fact they are usually designed so as to achieve the desired order.

The File and the Document

It is normally considered that as the size of a collection of documents increases, so must the degree of precision of the indexing, by use of either more entries or more precise terms, in order adequately to distinguish individual documents from each other and minimize effort for the searcher. Manly (1961) rebuts this idea, pointing out that the differentiation needed by the researcher is not from other documents in a collection, but from the rest of the universe of knowledge. While Manly's argument is certainly correct as far as it goes (and he does make clear that it does not apply to all kinds of information needs), he fails to consider costs at all. A major constraint on indexing is the cost of providing access, and an approach that adequately differentiates within a collection at least helps users at that level. To try to differentiate at the level recommended by Manly would be expensive and would also carry a high risk of error, since it requires the indexer to know the fields covered in more detail than can normally be the case.

Increasing the number of entries may improve access but it can also hinder satisfactory retrieval. There can come a point in highly exhaustive indexing where access is provided for minor ideas which are extremely unlikely to be useful. A similar problem reduces the effectiveness of pure Boolean search on text words (derivative indexing), since as the source of indexable matter grows larger, so does the number of minor words which become index entries.

The size of an index is typically set in some fashion, even if not in explicit terms. Whatever the storage medium may be, providing more of it will be costly, and a limit will be reached somewhere. Since the total size of the index is usually more or less limited, the designer must choose whether to provide a large number of simple access points, each with minimal information, or a smaller number that are highly precise and/or contain more information in the entry. The actual number of documents to be included can also be influenced by this need. Since these are within-collection constraints, the decision can best be made in terms of the collection. Enough access points should be provided to point out all the most important ideas in documents, at a level of precision high enough to differentiate the documents from each other, thus minimizing search effort.

Machine-readable storage very clearly influences the actual design of the index "document." Machine-readable form is so compact that far more can be stored—full text is becoming commonplace—while permitting search on a great many more access points. Very little information is actually stored with most of the entries in a machine record, but the computer performs the task of going from access point to full record so quickly and painlessly (in normal circumstances) that it is essentially invisible to the user.

The decision on number of entries may influence the characteristics of the syndetic structure, since it is possible to eliminate the necessity for downward cross-references by automatically posting all documents to the higher-level index terms from which the downward references would ordinarily be made (generic posting), as well as to the terms that describe them precisely. Similarly, "see" (use) references may be eliminated by duplicating entry under all term forms and synonyms. Generally, neither of these options is even considered for files held on paper or in microform because of the additional space they require. Usually the choice instead is to save costs by imposing an extra lookup on the user who happens not to select the preferred term. Indexes stored and searched in machine-readable form suffer less from the space constraint, and it is often perfectly possible to consider the other advantages and disadvantages of entry duplication without regard to space constraints.

In considering whether to substitute generic posting for downward cross-references, it is important to be aware that such a practice will result in the confounding of a great many documents on highly specific topics under the general terms, probably ill-serving the user who really wants a general document. The organization of the file provided by the reference structure is probably much more helpful in any except very small systems than the grouping of so many documents. Of course, generic posting can be a partial substitute for the references that are often omitted from a machine-held file. It would really be preferable to include the references in the file, however.

There is another factor to be considered in any system of duplicating entries, whether it be generic posting or synonymous entries. This is the issue of consistency. If entry is to be duplicated at all, it must be done for all applicable cases, because a user who finds some material that fills his or her need under an index heading will normally assume all such material is located there, and will not go and search under related or synonymous terms. With or without a reference (preferably with) there is at least a chance that the user who finds nothing will try elsewhere. If computer aids are available to duplicate entries automatically then duplication procedures are relatively safe; otherwise indexing procedures must be carefully designed to assure consistency.

The File and the Vocabulary: Physical Aspects

Purposes of the File

If the file is intended to provide current awareness, then compromises that increase the speed of availability of the index are appropriate even at the price of some other types of refinements. The most obvious of these compromises is use of derivative indexing. If the documents need not pass through a human indexing cyclo, they can be made available more quickly. Derivative indexing can have a positive advantage under these circumstances too in that there is no danger that the inflexibility of a controlled vocabulary will prevent entries from being made under new concepts as soon as they arise.

On the other hand, a file designed for retrospective reference needs vocabulary control because the scatter introduced by derivative indexing makes some searches extremely difficult; furthermore, it is difficult to provide adequate precision in breaking down large topics solely by use of derivative indexing. While fast availability is always desirable, it can be useful to spend a little more time on an index intended to be of permanent value. If a file is to be used for both current and retrospective purposes, it is therefore desirable to have both derived and assigned terms available. Fortunately this state of affairs is becoming common with the increased availability of machine search, but as long as printed tools are heavily used, the issue must still be faced. In a machine-search environment it may be desirable to put records online for current awareness search as soon as they are received, adding human indexing for retrospective search later.

Current awareness searches are typically fairly broad; retrospective ones may be broad or narrow. Even broad retrospective searches, however, are very rarely for everything on the broad subject; more often they are for a few documents that adequately show the state of the art. Thus, a file designed for retrospective search should be arranged in a fashion that makes it easy to zero in on a precise topic. The search for a few good documents on a broad topic will typically be satisfied by retrieval of some documents on the topic as a whole without locating those on its subtopics. The current awareness search, however, needs an arrangement that makes feasible the rapid scanning of a broad area. Since such a search does not cover a very long span and therefore will retrieve fewer documents, the fact that its precision is lower is not an unbearable handicap.

Alphabetic indexing usually serves retrospective needs, while a broad classification serves current awareness. Assuming the alphabetic terms are precise enough, the user can go directly to the one that covers the information desired, while broad classes bring together related documents for current awareness. Precise classification can serve both purposes, but it still requires alphabetical indexing to permit the specific topics of a retrospective search to be located.

If the file is intended to substitute where possible for physical access to items that are relatively inaccessible, then index access obviously needs to be at a more precise level than otherwise, leading to a near-requirement for information unit indexing in order to aid accurate judgment as to whether the item is of enough value to be worth the trouble of gaining access to it. Additionally, for the same purpose, as much information as possible should be carried with the entry.

Size Constraints

In derivative indexes, whether the added space required for use of a stoplist instead of a dictionary is warranted by the additional flexibility and access to new and/or rare terms must be decided in each different set of circumstances. The constraints of space, however, are likely to be the ruling factor. If enough space is available, the stoplist will most likely be used; if space is tight enough to warrant the extra processing and loss of information, a dictionary form is likely.

Space considerations also dominate the structure of assignment indexes that use complex terms. Ideally it would be possible to locate an item by searching under any significant element of its index term. With very complex, highly precise terms such as those found in many chain indexes it may well be desirable to be able to search on several different permutations of the elements of a term at the same access point if there are many entries at that access point. However, in printed or microform indexes it is essentially impossible to permute the elements of complex terms because the extra size is simply not cost-effective.

Chain indexing was invented to provide a predictable order for the elements in compound terms, thereby making it possible to avoid permuting the strings of elements. The technique has not been completely successful however, and other schemes, important among them PRECIS, have been designed to achieve the same goal. Terms in these systems become so complex primarily because they are intended to be fairly coextensive with the entire subject of the document.

Another trade-off that may be made to keep within size constraints is that between the coextensiveness of the terms and the amount of information given in the entry. The fundamental purpose of greater specification of terms is to permit the user to locate directly the precise topic of interest, while that of providing more information with the entry is to permit a better weeding out of irrelevant documents on the basis of this information. However, the ultimate goal for both is to minimize the total time and effort required to find the needed information, and it is possible to trade off coextensiveness in terms against provision of more information. For instance, a long string of index terms may substitute for provision of an abstract, or even of a title, with the entry. The reverse is also true. The trade-off comes in the fact that while the abstract may, and the title will certainly be available without separate intellectual input, the indexing typically requires a separate human intellectual operation. On the other hand, the title and abstract information do not contribute to arranging the items in the most useful order, whereas the indexing terms do (or at least are supposed to do so).

Pre- and Postcoordination

The choice between pre- and postcoordinate search interacts significantly with term and vocabulary design choices. If the document itself is the source of terms, then a useful precoordinate index will be difficult to develop. Even if essentially the same words are consistently used for the same topics throughout the collection (something that will rarely be true), the phrasing cannot be relied upon to be the same. Therefore, unless essentially all terms are precoordinated with all others, or some other arbitrary device is used, precoordination requires significant human editing of the derived entries.

For the same reason, if index terms are derived from the text, it is extremely difficult to develop a complex term structure, though it is relatively simple just to string the terms out after each other alphabetically or on the basis of the order of their occurrence in the text. Citation order becomes relatively unimportant in such a case; access must be provided to every term, but the nonmeaningful subarrangement means the entire string of elements must be scanned.

While they are not by any means synonymous, the choices between pre- and postcoordination and between enumeration and synthesis are very closely related. Synthesis in the usual sense means construction of the index term from available elements at input while postcoordination involves term synthesis at the output stage. Another difference is that in synthetic indexes the ways in which terms may be synthesized are typically limited by rules; with postcoordination any terms may be joined.

The analogy may also be applied to precoordinate and enumerative indexes; if the vocabulary is enumerative then all the combinations permissible in indexing are given in the vocabulary; in a precoordinate vocabulary all the combinations are already present.

Of course it is necessary to observe that this does not mean that precoordinate indexes are enumerative and postcoordinate ones are synthetic; the one refers to the index terms and the other to the structure of vocabulary. A precoordinate index may be synthetic, and a postcoordinate one may be enumerative.

Storage and Search Media

If computer search is to be used, then at least some of the terms may well be derived from the document, even if an external source is also used for assignment of controlled terms. Given this opportunity, the source of indexable matter for the derived terms at least can well be the entire machine-stored record. If the record is extremely large, for example, full text, it may be desirable to add frequency or other information to the record of at least some terms to permit more flexibility in retrieval.

Objective means (dictionary or stoplist) of term selection for derivative indexes are much more likely to be applied to a machine-stored form, whereas subjective means involving human marking of keywords will be used for manually operated files. The computer can search its dictionary very rapidly and efficiently; the equivalent operation for a human is relatively slow and tedious, so much so that a controlled vocabulary might as well be used. Similarly, many of the refinements to derivative indexing such as alteration of the terms, binding of terms to each other, and provision for subarrangement are all based on the need to make the index searchable by the human eye and/or to reduce the amount of space consumed in an eye-readable medium.

The need for complex structure in assigned terms arises from the same need—to provide an array a human can search conveniently, without consuming an undue amount of space. More flexibility is possible in computer search if the complex terms are decomposed into simpler ones. They can still be joined for search, but different combinations are possible. Perhaps best of all, the citation order of the elements in a complex term can become much less critical. It can still be helpful to be able to search on the terms of a controlled vocabulary, but the success of the index is not so dependent on their being in the "expected" alphabetical or notation location as long as a reference or some form of guidance is to be found at that location.

In the present state of the art the only derivative methods used for printed indexes are stoplists and dictionaries. Methods based on characteristics of the document or of the collection are used only in machine-searchable indexes. There is no evidence to indicate that this limitation has any basis in the limitations of the medium; rather it appears that researchers in these methods of retrieval have only been interested in machine search and therefore the work required to adapt them to printed formats has not been undertaken.

The medium also affects the refinements used in derivative indexes, because some of these have a strong influence on the physical size of the index. A stoplist-based derivative index that provides any form of permutation of terms will have so many entries that it will be constrained to give very little information with each entry. The choice must be based on consideration of whether the finer breakdown of the index entry compensates for the reduced amount of information provided.

Schuegraf (1980) suggests that the associative processors that are becoming available should affect the types of index terms used. The controlled vocabulary will consist only of very general terms used to partition the documents into groups small enough for associative search on the content of the documents. This suggestion applies, of course, only to the extent to which derivative indexing will serve the purposes of the index.

The layout and typography of the pages in a paper or microform index affects the kind of vocabulary structure that is feasible to use. The greater the flexibility available in typography and spacing, the more complexity may be introduced into the subject terms. For instance, in an index that starts each modifier on a new line, levels of modification may be differentiated by indentation, permitting use of more levels than in a run-on paragraph style, where even if complex punctuation conventions are used to differentiate levels of modification, they will be difficult to follow. In another kind of format, the indexes produced by the H. W. Wilson Company use variations of typeface and spacing on the line to differentiate levels of subdivision. The limitation of all these refinements is the human eye and brain, which must be able to grasp and remember them.

Coates (1976) analyzes the effect that the choice between cards and printed pages may have in evaluation (and therefore presumably usability) of indexes. While his specific concern was with the Cranfield study, which was based on card-form indexes, his points are broadly applicable. Typography and layout can break up pages into blocks of related entries. The page layout and vocabulary structure should interact with each other because the heading–subheading form works much better if typographic distinctions are available. Coates suggests that "user mobility"—the ability to scan a group of entries on a printed page—may be equivalent in value to, and of course much cheaper and faster than, consulting a thesaurus and rerunning a machine search.

The File and the Vocabulary: Intellectual Aspects

Syndetic Structure

A purely derivative system cannot provide syndetics because a syndetic structure cannot be derived from the words of a text any more than a classified arrangement can be. Words do not carry within themselves any consistent evidence regarding the relations among the concepts they denote. Most tools using derivative methods have no syndetic structure at all, but such works as the *Bibliography of Agriculture* demonstrate that this condition is not inherent in derivative indexing.

However, derivative indexing is limited in the amount of structure it can provide; furthermore, such systems are usually developed in order to minimize human intellectual input. Developing a sophisticated syndetic structure runs counter to this primary intent, and to the extent to which the indexing goes beyond the words of the document it ceases to be derivative. Furthermore, any term not treated in the syndetic structure—such as terms that have not appeared before—will of course have no aid to its location.

However, procedures for automatic generation of syndetics are improving, as may be seen in the work of Doszkocs (1978), Blackwell and Kochtanek (1981), and Preece (1981), and it seems reasonable to project that there is considerable promise in the application of such techniques to derivative indexes. If this projection is correct, then one of the major problems in derivative indexing—scatter of synonymous or closely related terms—will be considerably alleviated in the future.

The more highly constructed and complex the vocabulary, the more complex the syndetic structure required. A vocabulary composed exclusively of single words and simple direct phrases, for instance, requires "see" references only from synonyms and related terms. One that uses inversions, modifiers, etc., requires references not only from those, but from all the significant words not in the first position of a term and in general from the major alternative ways of expressing the concept. The point here is that the more possible ways of expressing a concept may be seen in the index, the more complex the required syndetic structure.

Arrangement

The means of arrangement is strongly related to the source of terms, whether internal or external to the documents. It is not possible to arrange a truly derivative index in classified order. While it would theoretically be possible to develop a classified order for the terms, this order would have to be imposed from outside; it could not be derived from the terms themselves, though as with the possibility of automatic generation of syndetic structure, future research developments may change this judgment.

In addition, in an alphabetically ordered derivative index any subarrangement on the basis of other than the more or less accidental co-occurrence of words requires that the terms be altered from their appearance in the text in order to achieve the intended subarrangement. For instance, hyphenation of word pairs may be used not only to prevent the second word of the pair from becoming an access point, but also to cause the pair to file in a separate sequence after all occurrences of the word alone.

The use of a classified arrangement also limits the language of the terms. By definition it must be a constructed one. True, the phrases describing the classes at each level may be in natural language, but the "term" is the artificial sequence of characters that is the basis for the location of the entry.

The Document and the Vocabulary

If derivative indexing is to be used, a larger source for indexable matter will make the operation far more difficult. There will be more text to process and the number of entries generated will be proportionately larger. The briefer parts of the text—titles, abstracts, captions, etc.—contain rather concentrated information and will therefore have a higher proportion of words that are highly indicative of the content of the document. It is really impractical to go much beyond titles in derivative indexes unless the machine-readable version is to be searched. In a printed or microform format, there would be far too many entries, inadequately differentiated. Storage for machine search can be far more compact, and this mode permits use of Boolean logic or other methods to refine retrieval.

In derivative indexes the choice of term selection method will also have a strong influence on the number of entries generated. A system relying on stoplists will produce a great many more entries for each document and therefore a larger index, other factors being equal, than one relying on a dictionary or on subjective means of term selection, because there will inevitably be many terms that would neither be individually common enough to place on a stoplist, nor valuable enough in indexing to warrant their inclusion in a go list or dictionary. These terms will therefore generate entries in a stoplist-based index, but not in the other types.

Summary

The choices examined in this chapter are those that cut across the three major sections of this book.

Size is generally a limiting factor in indexes, even when no explicit bounds are set. It may be measured in physical bulk, number of entries, number of characters, or some other criterion, but it affects a wide variety of decisions. For example, indexes may be produced in microform or even in machine-readable form only because they would be uneconomic in printed form. The reasons for not providing permuted entries in printed derivative indexes have to do with size—the large number of entries generated under each word and the physical size of the index.

The mode of search, while being influenced by the considerations of size mentioned above, also affects a variety of other choices, such as development of a syndetic structure, and use of derivative or assignment indexing. The kind of syndetic structure is also influenced by the arrangement, whether alphabetical or classified.

The degree of coextensiveness of terms affects a great many aspects of vocabulary design. As terms become more coextensive their breadth narrows, their number increases, and more permissiveness is required of the vocabulary. In addition, literary warrant must govern the addition of terms, and synthesis is almost required.

There are a number of interactions between the design of the file as a whole and the treatment of individual documents. Terms must at least adequately differentiate documents within the collection from each other, requiring more, or more precise, entries. Size enters in here, too, since the number of access points and the amount of information at each may be traded off against each other, at least in eye-readable systems. Decisions on duplication of entries may affect the characteristics of the syndetic structure.

The purposes (current awareness or retrospective search) for which a file is designed influence the type of vocabulary and the arrangement. Space considerations will influence the number of entries and the types of terms used, whether simple or complex, pre- or postcoordinate. The media of storage and search also influence decisions on source of terms, degree of structure in assigned terms, and refinements in derivative indexes. Layout of eye-readable indexes governs vocabulary structure.

The design of the file also interacts with the vocabulary design. Provision of syndetics requires some assignment of terms, as does a classified arrangement. However, automatic syndetic assignment and classification may in the future reduce the human intervention required.

Derivative indexing tends to produce a large number of entries. Using larger sources of indexable matter aggravates this tendency, as does use of certain term selection methods.

Case Study: Design of a Newspaper Index

The goal of this section is to show how the options described throughout this book were applied in an actual case, the design of a newspaper index. The collection was the *Washington Post* on microfilm, but beyond this, essentially all design factors were open.

The *Washington Post* is a major national newspaper with a possible 100,000 items of editorial content per year, plus many thousands of advertisements, which could conceivably be indexed. Like any newspaper it contains a wide variety of material. Articles range from a few lines to hundreds of column inches, and may cover literally any subject in the universe of human knowledge. They may represent opinion, reportage, or some combination of these; they may describe the latest developments or summarize well-known information. The articles may be accompanied by various kinds of pictorial or graphic material, while advertisements may be almost purely pictorial or graphic, purely text, or some mixture of the two.

While not all the information in a newspaper is truly "new," the emphasis is on providing knowledge of current events, and therefore the information may go out of date very quickly. The purpose of the index could not be current awareness—it had to be provided in hard copy, and when the information that is to be accessed is as topical as the news, then any service that requires another pass through a printing press cannot be considered a true current awareness service.

Accessibility of the original items was expected to be relatively limited. Newspapers are widely disseminated and quickly discarded. Even when it is desirable that they be maintained, the nature of the medium discourages this—the size is very unwieldy and a low-grade quality of paper is used that disintegrates rapidly.

Thus access must be to a reproduction, usually and in the case of the *Washington Post Index*, in microform. It was anticipated that the index would be disseminated more widely than the film, meaning that in some locations the originals would be relatively inaccessible.

Since permanent retrospective access to a relatively inaccessible collection was intended, it was important to provide as much help as possible in sorting out nonuseful documents within the entry itself. Reporting in a newspaper of an event or issue may involve many stories over a long period of time. These stories often cannot realistically be differentiated by means of index terms; the most practical way to distinguish them is to provide some sort of annotation or abstract, and brief abstracts were chosen for this index. For the same reason, high-quality human indexing with a controlled vocabulary had to be used. The only bibliographic information provided to identify a specific item was its locator—date, section, page, and column. Byline and headline would have added a great many more characters without commensurate increase in information provision. In fact, this decision may be seen as a trade-off against specification of subject by means of provision of brief abstracts—a similar amount of space is consumed, but the abstract, being specifically designed for its purpose, can convey more information about the actual content of the item.

Two other items of information were provided to aid in sorting out useful articles: (1) an indication of length (under one-half column, up to one column, over one column); and (2) types of illustrations attached to the article. Thus, particularly for issue rather than event reporting, a user could select articles that had a high likelihood of being comprehensive, and if illustrative material was desired, articles containing pictures, charts, etc., could be selected.

As might be expected, it was economically infeasible to reproduce the article with the index entry; hence a minimum of two lookups was required. In order to save space a third lookup was often imposed on users: whenever the same article required access under two related subjects, entry was made under one with a reference from the other, requiring users who first searched under the second subject to refer to the first one before going to the original.

The dominant use of the index for the foreseeable future was to be human search of hard copy, requiring that the index terms be designed to provide enough differentiation to permit selection of probably-useful items on the basis of a single index term. There was no compelling reason to use multiple files; in order to avoid confusing users, all entries were interfiled in a single alphabet.

As noted above, the primary storage medium selected was paper, though the index was also computer-stored with the intent (later realized) of making machine search possible. The index had to be available in a variety of locations, not all of which would have computer access. Microform was not seen as a viable alternative, and of course cards could not be used for a product designed for wide distribution. Given the requirement for availability in print, precoordinate search was also required.

Shorter entries—that is, entries without annotations—would have permitted loosening of the size restriction on articles and/or an increase in the number of entries per article. The latter would have been a near certainty, since the reason for using references in preference to entries in many cases was the space required on the printed page for the abstract.

Alphabetical arrangement of subject terms, with chronological arrangement of items that were indexed by the same subheadings, was adopted. It would be very difficult, if not impossible, to design a classification that would cover the varied and changing subjects of newspaper articles. The upfront investment to develop such a tool would be prohibitive, and existing classifications would not provide an appropriate balance of detail to suit the collection. Even if it were possible to develop a classification, the task of updating it to cover rapid development of news topics would be both costly and slow. While the goal of the index was to aid retrospective search, retrospective in the context of the news implies a much less leisurely pace than might be the case with other types of collections.

A syndetic structure was developed in order to provide some of the same forms of access that classification would have permitted. A relatively simple structure was adopted, based on both economic constraints and analysis of the expected user groups and the collection. The index had to be accessible to all levels of users and its syndetic structure should not bewilder or confuse them; furthermore, the rapidly evolving nature of the news meant that developing and maintaining a complex structure would have caused much the same problems as use of a classification, discussed above.

Development of the structure was at first entirely manual because computer facilities were not fully developed; later some machine aids were provided, but their limits were those of the computer system.

In a general sense, of course, the collection to be indexed was the newspaper. However, not every discrete item—every ad, every brief article, every column, every comic strip—could or should be covered. While any of these could conceivably be a target of search at some time, the likelihood of many of them being wanted very often was extremely low. At the same time the index had to be produced at a price that would make it possible for libraries to purchase it.

Therefore, the collection would not consist of every item in the paper. The unique material in a newspaper is obviously the news, and the criterion for deciding on selection of items was therefore their news value. All articles, editorials, and commentaries exceeding a minimum length of 2½ inches were included. Question and answer and how-to columns were omitted; these are normally not news and contain information that is readily available in other sources. Advertisements of news value were also included; deciding what made an ad newsworthy was one of the major challenges of designing the index. In the end the criteria developed were (1) if the ad was sponsored by a corporation or other preexisting organization, it must have content that would not be routinely expected as part of the public relations effort of the organization; or (2) ads sponsored by individuals or ad hoc groups must be sponsored or signed by prominent individuals.

While comic strips do make the news, this is rare and unpredictable; indexing the subjects of comic strips was simply not feasible. In any case, an article (which would be indexed) referring to a particular strip would generally give the day on which it appeared, or even reproduce it, so that an index entry for the strip itself would not be vital.

Sports presented another problem. In the original design of the index, sports events were treated like any other news, but it became evident that we were simply filling up the index with lists of scores and winners. There are adequate tools available to look up dates of sports events and their results; once the date is known the user does not need an index to know on what date it would be reported in the paper, though it will be necessary to search the sports section to find the article.

Certain other exclusions, primarily of material deemed of purely local interest, were made for the sake of economy. Routine crime reports that appeared not to have broader impact were omitted. The justification for this practice is purely one of economy and judgment about uses to be made of the index, because access to this information, unlike sports information, is not so readily available from other sources. However, the index was directed at a national audience, whose interest in every robbery reported in Washington, D. C. and environs was assumed to be minimal.

The source of indexable matter was the entire article, though with concentration on the first few paragraphs. Use of headlines was minimized because these are so often incomplete or even misleading. Newspaper articles are usually short compared to journal articles, let alone books; furthermoro it is not unusual for a report on a second subject to be tacked on to the end of an article. Hence the entire article was indexed. Byline entries were made only for a few well-known commentators.

The unit of indexable information was normally the entire article, though on occasion an article might be divisible into two parts, each of which should be indexed. No effort was made to provide information unit indexing, however.

Within the constraints of bibliographic unit indexing, there was no limit on the number of entries. However, entering essentially the same information in more than one place was avoided due to the length of the annotations that were provided with each entry. Cross-references were freely used instead.

Realistically, term assignment had to be used. As noted above, headlines are frequently incomplete or misleading; they certainly could not be used as the source of derived terms. Resources were not available to deal with the machine-readable form of the paper, and there was no machine-readable version that matched the printed copy. Even had it been available, development of the sophisticated systems that would be required to produce a usable printed index from the full text would have required an unacceptably large allocation of both time and resources.

Modified natural language was chosen for terms; a constructed language had already been rejected, as previously discussed. A moderate degree of term complexity was required in order to achieve adequate specification of subjects. Coextensiveness at the article level was not attempted; the common type of entry grouping is a series of articles describing the development of a story over time, and this development is usually best shown in chronological order. However, an attempt was made to provide a reasonable degree of coextensiveness at the story level, to differentiate stories from each other.

In the design of the vocabulary authority, literary warrant was used exclusively for addition of terms to the vocabulary, with some consideration of the structure of knowledge in development of the syndetics. While the news may cover any subject, the areas being emphasized are quite variable. To use the structure of knowledge in designing the vocabulary would mean developing a universal authority, only a small portion of which would ever be used.

The vocabulary enumerated all simple concepts and those complex ones that did not recur throughout the system. Synthesis was used for concepts that recurred frequently in conjunction with other concepts. The vocabulary had to be highly permissive because the need for new terms was a continuing one.

Since it was known that many entries would be generated under a single access point for the frequent major continuing stories, and that most of the stories would be about a single event or series of events, the decision was to provide a precise breakdown, even at the expense of having fewer entries for each article. This required a larger number of cross-references to provide for other needed access points.

The flexibility available in computer typesetting made the use of highly structured terms feasible. These same structures, however, also mandated the extensive syndetics that were developed.

The fundamental criteria that constrained other decisions in design of this index may be seen as:

1. production in printed form,
2. relatively large amount of information with each entry,
3. precise subject term breakdowns, and
4. concentration on retrospective access.

These criteria grew out of certain independent variables:

1. unavailability of computer access to many prospective users,
2. relative inaccessibility of the original documents,
3. large number of items to be expected under a single access point, and
4. extreme currency of the news.

Epilogue

It is common to think and speak of many of the factors in design of indexing systems as though they were separable from each other—for example, to consider the source of indexable matter apart from the source of terms or the arrangement. Yet these choices and others strongly influence each other, in some cases so strongly that one decision may literally predetermine another.

Indexing is often considered with some reverence in speech but accorded far less importance in practice. Yet, whenever a collection of information, by reason of its size, its location, or the medium on which it is stored, cannot conveniently be scanned in its entirety by any would-be user, the quality of its index determines its value perhaps more than any other factor.

It is well known that most seekers after information will prefer easily available information of lesser quality to that which is more difficult to reach, even though it may be of higher quality, at least in satisfying the need of the moment. Part of the reason for this tendency may be the high level of uncertainty regarding the value of a particular item. In most cases, unless the surrogate is very extensive—for example, a good informative abstract—it is necessary to examine the original in order to make a final determination as to whether it will be of value. Naturally there is a tendency, if access to the original will be difficult, to rationalize that it is probably of limited value anyway, and hence not worth the trouble of pursuit.

Unfortunately, providing access to information is not cheap, and not all information is so valuable that it is worth the cost of providing easy access. Everyone knows this; the problem is that we have to date done very poorly in our attempts to place concrete values on information and therefore on providing access to it. The closest we have come is to find out with variable reliability what people are willing to pay (or say they are willing to pay) for access. This is not the same thing as the value of the information, unless one assumes the potential users know the worth of information before they get it. In many cases they would be hard put to it to assign a concrete value even after acquiring the information.

This book is not designed to fill this particular gap in our knowledge. That would be the province of a vastly different work, or rather a whole series of them. Instead, the goal here has been to help the designer who has decided that making a body of information available is worth a certain expenditure of resources to assure that access is maximized for this expenditure.

The approach taken is a variant of the total-system approach. Little attempt has been made to quantify variables, many of which are not all that quantifiable anyway in the present state of the art. Instead, the indexing process has been treated as a group of interrelated variables and decisions. The effect of each part of the index system on the other parts of the system has been examined. Without this approach it is all too easy to cause severe harm to one part of a system by "improving" another without careful examination of the impact of the improvement.

If this book may be used by index designers to produce indexes which serve their intended purposes well and economically it will have achieved its primary goal.

References

Abbot, M. T. J.; Hunter, P. S.; Simkins, M. A. "Current Awareness Searches on CT, CBAC, and ASCA." Aslib Proceedings 20(2):129–143, February 1968.

Aitchison, Jean. "The Thesaurofacet: A Multipurpose Retrieval Language Tool." Journal of Documentation 26(3):187–203, September 1970.

Aitchison, Jean; Gomersall, Alan; Ireland, Ralph. Thesaurofacet: A Thesaurus and Faceted Classification for Engineering and Related Subjects. Whetstone, Leicester, England: English Electric Co., 1969.

Aitchison, Jean; Gilchrist, Alan. Thesaurus Construction: A Practical Manual. London: Aslib, 1972.

American Library Association. Rules for Filing Catalog Cards (2nd ed.). Chicago: American Library Association, 1968.

American National Standards Institute. American National Standard Guidelines for Thesaurus Structure, Construction, and Use. New York: American National Standards Institute, 1973. (ANS Z39.19–1974)

American National Standards Institute. USA Standard Basic Criteria for Indexes. New York: American National Standards Institute, 1974. (ANS Z39.4–1974)

American National Standards Institute. American National Standard for Bibliographic References. New York: American National Standards Institute, 1977. (ANS Z39.29–1977)

American Records Management Association. Rules for Alphabetical Filing as Standardized by the Association. Detroit: American Records Management Association, 1960.

Anglo-American Cataloguing Rules. Prepared by the American Library Association, the British Library, the Canadian Committee on Cataloguing, the Library Association, the Library of Congress; edited by Michael Gorman and Paul W. Winkler (2nd ed.). Chicago: American Library Association, 1978.

Artandi, Susan; Hines, Theodore C. "Roles and Links—or Forward to Cutter." American Documentation, 14(1): 74–77, January 1963.

Besterman, Theodore. The Beginnings of Systematic Bibliography (2nd ed.). New York: Burt Franklin, 1968.

Bird, P. R. "The Distribution of Indexing Depth in Documentation Systems." Journal of Documentation, 30(4): 381–390, December 1974.

Blackwell, Paul K.; Kochtanek, Thomas R. "An Iterative Technique for Document Retrieval Using Descriptors and Relators." Proceedings of the American Society for Information Science, 44th annual meeting, 1981, pp. 215–217.

194

Blagden, J. F. "How Much Noise in a Role-Free and Link-Free Co-ordinate Indexing System?" *Journal of Documentation*, 22(3):203–209, September 1966.

Blagden, J. F. "Thesaurus Compilation Methods: A Literature Review." *Aslib Proceedings*, 20(8):345–359, August 1968.

Bookstein, Abraham. "Fuzzy Requests: An Approach to Weighted Boolean Searches." *Journal of the American Society for Information Science*, 31(4):240–247, July 1980.

Borko, Harold. "Measuring the Reliability of Subject Classification by Men and Machines." *American Documentation*, 15(4):268–273, October 1964.

Borko, Harold; Bernier, Charles. *Abstracting Concepts and Methods*. New York: Academic Press, 1975.

Borko, Harold; Bernier, Charles. *Indexing Concepts and Methods*. New York: Academic Press, 1978.

Bourne, Charles P. "Initial Article Filing in Computer-Based Book Catalogs: Techniques, Problems and Article Frequencies." *Journal of Library Automation*, 8(3): 221–247, September 1975.

British Standards Institution. *Specification for Alphabetical Arrangement and the Filing Order of Numerals and Symbols*. London: British Standards Institution, 1969. (BS 1749:1969)

British Standards Institution. *Guidelines for the Establishment and Development of Monolingual Thesauri*. London: British Standards Institution, 1979. (BS 5723:1979)

Burnett, John E.; Cooper, David; Lynch, Michael F.; Willett, Peter; Wycherley, Maureen. "Document Retrieval Experiments Using Indexing Vocabularies of Varying Size. I. Variety Generation Symbols Assigned to the Fronts of Index Terms." *Journal of Documentation*, 35(3):197–206, September 1979.

Burress, Elaine P. "Automated Indexing Versus KWOC: A Performance Comparison." *Journal of the American Society for Information Science*, 31(1):60–61, January 1980.

Campey, Lucille H. "Costs of Producing KWIC/KWOC Indexes." *Information Storage and Retrieval*, 10(9/10):293–307, September/October 1974.

Cartwright, Kelley L. "Mechanization and Library Filing Rules." In *Advances in Librarianship*, Melvin Voigt (ed.). New York: Academic Press, 1970, pp. 59–94.

Coates, E. J. *Subject Catalogues: Headings and Structure*. London: Library Association, 1960.

Coates, E. J. "Card Indexes or Printed Pages—Physical Substrates in Index Evaluation." *Indexer*, 10(2):60–68, October 1976.

Coates, E. J. "Progress in Documentation: Some Properties of Relationships in the Structure of Indexing Languages." *Journal of Documentation*, 29(4):390–404, December 1973.

Collison, Robert L. *Indexes and Indexing* (4th rev. ed.). London: Ernest Benn, 1972.

Craven, Timothy C. "Automatic NEPHIS Coding of Descriptive Titles for Permuted Index Generation." *Journal of the American Society for Information Science*, 33(2):97–101, March 1982.

Cutter, Charles A. *Rules for a Dictionary Catalog* (4th ed.). Washington: Government Printing Office, 1904.

Daly, Lloyd W. *Contributions to a History of Alphabetization in Antiquity and the Middle Ages*. Brussels, Belgium: Latomus, 1967.

DeJong-Hofman, M. W. "Computer-Aided Searching in the INSPEC Data-base." *Online Review*, 2(2):175–198, June 1978.

Dolby, James L.; Resnikoff, H. L. "ACCESS: A Study of Information Storage and Retrieval with Emphasis on Library Information Systems." Washington: Department of Health, Education, and Welfare, March 1972. (Final report, Project no. 8–0548)

Doszkocs, Tamas E. "An Associative Interactive Dictionary (AID) for Online Bibliographic Searching." *Proceedings of the American Society for Information Science*, 41st annual meeting, 1978, pp. 105–109.

Elchesen, Dennis R. "Cost-Effectiveness Comparison of Manual and On-Line Retrospective Bibliographic Searching." *Journal of the American Society for Information Science*, 29(2):56–66, March 1978.

Feinberg, Hilda. *Title Derivative Indexing Techniques: A Comparative Study*. Metuchen, NJ: Scarecrow, 1973.

Fenichel, Carol. "Editing the Permuterm Subject Index." *Proceedings of the American Society for Information Science*, 34th annual meeting, 1971, pp. 349–353.

Field, B. J. "Towards Automatic Indexing. Vol. 1: Relationship Between Free- and Controlled-Language Indexing and the Automatic Generation of Controlled Subject Headings and Classifications." London: Inspec, 1975. (Report R75/20)

"Filing: Projects and Publications." *International Cataloguing*, 3(4):4–8, October/December 1974.

Fischer, Marguerite. "KWIC Index Concept: A Retrospective View." *American Documentation*, 17(2):57–70, April 1966.

Foskett, A. C. *The Subject Approach to Information* (3rd ed.). Hamden, CT: Linnet, 1977.

Friedman, H. A. *Newspaper Indexing*. Milwaukee: Marquette University Press, 1942.

Garfield, Eugene. "The Permuterm Subject Index: An Autobiographical Review." *Journal of the American Society for Information Science*, 27(5/6):288–291, September/October 1976.

Gifford, Carolyn; Baumanis, George J. "On Understanding User Choices: Textual Correlates of Relevance Judgements." *American Documentation*, 20(1): 21–26, January 1969.

Gilchrist, Alan. *The Thesaurus in Retrieval*. London: Aslib, 1971.

Gratch, Bonnie; Settel, Barbara; Atherton, Pauline. "Characteristics of Book Indexes for Subject Retrieval in the Humanities and Social Sciences." *Indexer*, 11(1):14–23, April 1978.

Hamill, Karen A.; Zamora, Antonio. "The Use of Titles for Automatic Document Classification." *Journal of the American Society for Information Science*, 31(6):396–402, November 1980.

Hartley, James; Davies, Lindsey; Burnhill, Peter. "Alphabetization in Indexes: Experimental Studies." *Indexer*, 12(3):149–153, April 1981.

Henzler, R. G. "Free or Controlled Vocabularies: Some Statistical User-Oriented Evaluations of Biomedical Information Systems." *International Classification*, 5(1):21–26, March 1978.

Hines, Theodore C. *The Collectanea as a Bibliographical Tool*. New Brunswick, NJ: Rutgers University, 1961. (Ph.D dissertation)

Hirayama, Kenzo. "Length of an Abstract and Amount of Information." *Journal of Chemical Documentation*, 4(1):9–11, 1964.

Hodges, Pauline R. "Keyword in Title Indexes: Effectiveness of Retrieval in Computer Searches." *Special Libraries*, 74(1):56–60, January 1983.

Hulme, E. Wyndham. "Principles of Book Classification (Chapter III)." *Library Association Record*, 13:446–447, 1911.

Hunt, Roslyn; Horne, C. Robin; Boone, Lucille; Dennis, Lyndal; Whelan, Helen. "PRECIS, LCSH and KWOC: Report of a Research Project Designed to Examine the Applicability of PRECIS to the Subject Catalogue of an Academic Library." Wollongong, Australia: University of Wollongong Library, 1976–1978. 14 microfiche. (Wollongong University Subject Catalogue Study)

Kaiser, J. *Systematic Indexing*. London: Pitman, 1911.

Kaiser, J. "Systematic Indexing." *Report of Proceedings of the Association of Special Libraries and Information Bureaux*, 3rd conference, London, 1926, pp. 20–33.

Keen E. Michael. "Document Length." In *Information Storage and Retrieval*. Department of Computer Science, Cornell University, 1968. (Scientific report no. ISR–13, p. V1– V60)

Keen, E. Michael. "On the Generation and Searching of Entries in Printed Subject Indexes." *Journal of Documentation*, 33(1):15–45, March 1977.

Kilgour, Frederick G., ed. *Library and Information Science CumIndex*. Los Altos, CA: R & D Press, 1972.

Kim, Chai. "Retrieval Language of Social Sciences and Natural Sciences: A Statistical Investigation." *Journal of the American Society for Information Science*, 33(1):3–7, January 1982.

Klingbiel, Paul H. "Machine-Aided Indexing of Technical Literature." *Information Storage and Retrieval*, 9:79–84, February 1973.

Klingbiel, Paul H.; Rinker, C. C. "Evaluation of Machine-Aided Indexing." *Information Processing and Management*, 12(6):351–366, 1976.

Knable, John. "Experiment Comparing Key Words Found in Indexes and Abstracts Prepared by Humans with Those in Titles." *American Documentation*, 16(2):123–124, April 1965.

Knight, G. Norman. "Book Indexing in Great Britain: A Brief History." *Indexer*, 6(1):14– 18, Spring 1968.

Lancaster, F. Wilfrid. "On the Need for Role Indicators in Postcoordinate Retrieval Systems." *American Documentation*, 19(1):42–46, January 1968.

Lancaster, F. Wilfrid. *Vocabulary Control for Information Retrieval*. Washington: Information Resources Press, 1972.

Landau, Herbert B. "Cost Analysis of Document Surrogation; A Literature Review." *American Documentation*, 20(4): 302–310, October 1969.

Langridge, Derek W. "Use of Classification in Book Indexing." *Indexer*, 2(3):95–98, Spring 1961.

Lefever, Maureen. "Managing an Uncontrolled Vocabulary Ex Post Facto; Addendum." *Journal of the American Society for Information Science*, 24(3):234, May 1973.

Lefever, Maureen; Freedman, Barbara; Schultz, Louise. "Managing an Uncontrolled Vocabulary Ex Post Facto." *Journal of the American Society for Information Science*, 23(6):339–342, November/December 1972.

Levine, Emil H. "Effect of Instantaneous Retrieval on Indexing Criteria." *Journal of the American Society for Information Science*, 25(3):199–200, May/June 1974.

Lilley, Oliver L. *Terminology, Form, Specificity and the Syndetic Structure of Subject Headings for English Literature*. New York: Columbia University, 1959. (D.L.S. dissertation)

Manly, Ron. "The Inadequacy of Varying the Depth of Indexing and other 'Document Collection' Approaches to Information Retrieval for Researchers." *American Documentation*, 12(3):204–205, July 1961.

Maloney, Ruth K. "Title Versus Title/Abstract Text Searching in SDI Systems." *Journal of the American Society for Information Science*, 25(6): 370–373, November/December 1974.

Maron, M. E. "Depth of Indexing." *Journal of the American Society for Information Science*, 30(4):224–228, July 1979.

Metcalfe, John W. *Information Retrieval, British and American, 1876–1976*. Metuchen, NJ: Scarecrow, 1976.

Miksa, Francis. *The Subject in the Dictionary Catalog from Cutter to the Present*. Chicago: American Library Association, 1983.

198

References

Milstead, Jessica L. "Natural Versus Inverted Word Order in Subject Headings." *Library Resources and Technical Services*, 24(2): 174–178, Spring 1980.

Mischo, William H. "Expanded Subject Access to Reference Collection Materials." *Journal of Library Automation*, 12(4): 338–354, December 1979.

Montague, Barbara A. "Testing, Comparison, and Evaluation of Recall, Relevance, and Cost of Coordinate Indexing with Links and Roles." *American Documentation*, 16(3): 201–208, July 1965.

Neufeld, M. Lynne; Graham, Kim L.; Mazella, Angela. "Machine-Aided Title Word Indexing for a Weekly Current Awareness Publication." *Information Processing and Management*, 10(11/12):403–410, November/December 1974.

Norris, Dorothy M. *A History of Cataloguing and Cataloguing Methods, 1100–1850*. London: Grafton, 1939.

Petrarca, Anthony E.; Lay, W. Michael. "The Double-KWIC Coordinate Index." *Journal of Chemical Documentation*, 9(4):256–261, November 1969.

Perez, Ernest. "Text Enhancement: Controlled Vocabulary vs. Free Text." *Special Libraries*, 73(3):183–192, July 1982.

Preece, Scott E. "Associative Searching by Spreading Activation." *Proceedings of the American Society for Information Science*, 44th annual meeting, 1981, pp. 331–332.

Prévost, Marie Louise. "An Approach to Theory and Method in General Subject Heading." *Library Quarterly*, 16:140–151, April 1946.

Raghavan, K. W.; Iyer, Hemalata. "Structuring of Compound and Complex Subjects in Social Sciences: A Users' Survey." *International Classification*, 5(1):8–14, 1978.

Richmond, Phyllis A. "Cats: An Example of Concealed Classification in Subject Headings." *Library Resources and Technical Services*, 3(2):102–112, Spring 1959.

Richmond, Phyllis A. "Classification from PRECIS: Some Possibilities." *Journal of the American Society for Information Science*, 27(4):240–247, July–August 1976.

Rolling, Loll. "Graphic Display Devices in Thesaurus Construction and Use." *Aslib Proceedings*, 23(11):591–594, November 1971.

Ryan, Vincent J.; Dearing, Vinton A. "Computerized Text Editing and Processing with Built-in Indexing." *Information Storage and Retrieval*, 10:211–228, May–June 1974.

Salton, Gerard; Wong, A. "Automatic Indexing Using Term Discrimination and Term Precision Measurements." *Information Processing and Management*, 12(1):43–51, 1976.

Salton, Gerard. *Dynamic Library and Information Processing*. Englewood Cliffs, NJ: Prentice-Hall, 1975.

Saraevic, Tefko. "Comparative Effects of Titles, Abstracts and Full Text on Relevance Judgments." *Proceedings of the American Society for Information Science*, 32nd annual meeting, 1969, pp. 293–299.

Sayers, W. C. Berwick. *Sayers' Manual of Classification for Librarians* (5th ed. by Arthur Maltby). London: Andre Deutsch, 1975.

Schuegraf, Ernst. "Indexing for Associative Processing." *Canadian Journal of Information Science*, 5:93–101, May 1980.

Seely, Barbara J. "Indexing Depth and Retrieval Effectiveness." *Drexel Library Quarterly*, 8(2):201–208, April 1972.

Sharp, John R. "SLIC Index." *American Documentation*, 17(1):41–44, January 1966.

Shores, J. Harlan. "An Empirical Study of the Use of a Letter by Letter and a Word by Word Index with Elementary School Children." (Unpublished manuscript, n.d.)

Soergel, Dagobert. *Indexing Languages and Thesauri: Construction and Maintenance*. Los Angeles: Melville, 1974.

Sparck Jones, Karen. "Automatic Classification." In Maltby, Arthur, ed., *Classification in the 1970s: A Second Look* (Rev. ed.). Hamden, CT: Linnet, 1976, pp. 209–225.

Sparck Jones, Karen. "Index Term Weighting." *Information Storage and Retrieval*, 9:619–633, November 1973.

Sparck Jones, Karen. "Progress in Documentation: Automatic Indexing." *Journal of Documentation*, 30(4): 393–432, December 1974.

"Superindex Test Program." Boca Raton, FL, 1982? (Unpublished report)

Surace, Cecily J. "The Displays of a Thesaurus." Santa Monica, CA: Rand Corp., March 1970. (ED 039002)

Svenonius, Elaine. "Use of Classification in Online Retrieval." *Library Resources and Technical Services*, 27(1):76–80, January–March 1983.

Swift, Donald F.; Winn, Viola A.; Bramer, Dawn A. "A Sociological Approach to the Design of Information Systems." *Journal of the American Society for Information Science*, 30(4):215–223, July 1979.

Taube, Mortimer. "Notes on the Use of Roles and Links in Coordinate Indexing." *American Documentation*, 12(2):98–100, April 1961.

Thompson, Charles W. N. "Functions of Abstracts in the Initial Screening of Technical Documents by the User." *Journal of the American Society for Information Science*, 24(4):270–276, July 1973.

Thompson, Mary. "The Letter of the Lore." *Australian Library Journal*, 25(6):196–198, June 1976.

Van Rijsbergen, Carl. "Automatic Classification in Information Retrieval." *Drexel Library Quarterly*, 14(2):75–89, April 1978.

Verner, Mathilde. "Adrien Baillet (1649–1706) and his Rules for an Alphabetic Subject Catalog." *Library Quarterly*, 38(3): 217–230, July 1968.

Vickery, Brian C. "Notational Symbols in Classification." *Journal of Documentation*, 8(1): 14–32, March 1952.

Vickery, Brian C. "Notational Symbols in Classification. Part II: Notation as an Ordering Device." *Journal of Documentation*, 12(2): 73–87, June 1956.

Vickery, Brian C. "Notational Symbols in Classification. Part III: Further Comparisons of Brevity." *Journal of Documentation*, 13:(2): 72–77, June 1957.

Vickery, Brian C. *Faceted Classification*. London: Aslib, 1960.

Vickery, Brian C. "Structure and Function in Retrieval Languages." *Journal of Documentation*, 27(2): 69–82, June 1971.

Vickery, Brian C. *Classification and Indexing in Science* (3rd ed.). London: Butterworth, 1975.

Vickery, Brian C. "Classificatory Principles in Natural Language Indexing Systems." Maltby, Arthur, ed., *Classification in the 1970s, a Second Look* (Rev. ed.). Hamden, CT: Shoe String, 1976, pp. 119–141.

Weinberg, Bella Hass. *Word Frequency and Automatic Indexing*. New York: Columbia University, 1981. (D.L.S. dissertation)

Wellisch, Hans H. "The Alphabetization of Prepositions in Indexes." *Indexer*, 12(2):90–92, October 1980(a).

Wellisch, Hans H. *Indexing and Abstracting: An International Bibliography*. Santa Barbara, CA: ABC-Clio, 1980(b).

Willett, Peter. "Document Retrieval Experiments Using Indexing Vocabularies of Varying Size. II. Hashing, Truncation, Digram and Trigram Encoding of Index Terms." *Journal of Documentation*, 35(4):296–305, December 1979.

Williams, Martha E. "Use of Machine-Readable Data Bases." In Cuadra, Carlos A.; Luke,

Ann, eds., *Annual Review of Information Science and Technology, Volume 9*. Washington: American Society for Information Science, 1974, pp. 221–284.

Witty, Francis J. "The Beginnings of Indexing and Abstracting: Some Notes Towards a History of Indexing and Abstracting in Antiquity and the Middle Ages." *Indexer*, 8(4):193–198, October 1973.

Working Party on Computer Filing Rules. "Filing by Computer: Report." *Catalogue and Index*, 27:1–16, Autumn 1972.

Yerkey, A. Neil. "Models of Index Searching and Retrieval Effectiveness of Keyword-in-Context Indexes." *Journal of the American Society for Information Science*, 24(4):282–286, July/August 1973.

Index

Indexers
 penalized for work, 8
 professional, origin, 9
Indexes, see specific types of indexes, e.g.
 Computer-readable indexes; Postcoordinate indexing; and indexes to specific types of materials, e.g. Books,
 indexing
Indexing, see also Subject access systems;
 and specific aspects of subject, e.g.
 Depth of indexing
 compared with other subject access
 methods, 3–4, 85, 93
Indexing languages, see Controlled
 vocabularies; Subject headings
Information, see also specific topics, e.g.
 Scattering of information
 amount carried with entry, 24, 170–171,
 186–187
 computer search needs, 171–172
 relationships
 accessibility of original, 25–26, 27,
 178
 number of access points, 176
 size of classification categories, 59
 storage costs, 37
 term coextensiveness,179
Information retrieval, computer-based,
 see Computer search
Information unit indexing, 93–95, 98, 178
Input costs, derivative and assignment indexing, 105–107, 110–111, 116–117
Input/output volume, choice of term
 source, 116–117
INSPEC database, 116, 117
Interfiling of pre-existing indexes, 12, 88,
 95, 96
International Organisation for Standardisation, 47
Inversion of index terms, 61, 62, 69–70,
 138–140, 141–142
Inverted file organization, 37–38
Item on term indexes, 29, 37, 42

J

Jewett, Charles C., 9
Journal articles, indexing, 8, 87–88, 94–95
 compared with book cataloguing, 4
 history, 104
 title words, 92

K

Kaiser, J., 10, 142, 159
Keen, E. Michael, 92, 153
Keyword in context indexing, see KWIC
 indexing
Keyword indexing
 amount of information in entry, 21
 history, 7, 104–105
 library catalogues, 9
 syndetic structure, 71
 titles, 92
Keyword out of context indexing, see
 KWOC indexing
Kilgour, Frederick G., 88, 96
Kim, Chai, 124
Klingbiel, Paul H., 123
Knable, John, 92
Knight, G. Norman, 8, 9
Knowledge, effects of structure and
 growth, 155–157, 161–162, 164, 175
KWIC indexing, 11, 104–105, 120
 format, 130–131
 subarrangement, 108–109
KWOC indexing, 115
 format, 130–131
 recall performance, 114

L

Lamoignon, Chrétien-François de, 8
Lancaster, F. Wilfrid, 34, 35, 69, 116–117,
 156
Laudau, Herbert B., 35
Langridge, Derek W., 64
Languages, indexing, see Controlled
 vocabularies
Languages of collections, 87
Lefever, Maureen, 107, 127
Letter by letter arrangement, 48–50
Levine, Emil H., 27
Library catalogues, see Catalogues
Library collections, indexable matter, 94
Library of Congress Classification, 158
Library of Congress Subject Headings,
 10, 139, 156, 162, see also Subject
 headings
Lilley, Oliver L., 141
Links and roles, 34–35, 151–152
Literary warrant, 155–157, 164, 175, 190
Locators, 9–10, 19–22, 63, 187

Permuterm Subject Index, 107, 122, 123, 132, 150
Petrarca, Anthony E., 132
Political Science Thesaurus, 124
Poole's periodical index, 104
Postcoordinate classification, 58
Postcoordinate indexing, 10, 29, 33–36, 41–42
  links and roles, 34–35, 151–152
  term structure, 147, 148, 151–152
  Uniterms, 121
Postcoordinate search, 171, 179–180
PRECIS, 35, 64, 115, 150
Precision, see Recall and precision
Precoordinate classification, 58
Precoordinate indexing, 33–36, 142, 143–151
Precoordinate search, 171, 179–180
Predictability of index terms, 142–143
Preece, Scott E., 183
Prefatory matter, as indexable matter source, 90
Prefixes, arrangement, 50
Prepositions, 140–141
  arrangement, 55
Prescriptive cross references, 70, 71, 73–75, see also Syndetic structure
Prescriptiveness, index vocabularies, 160–163, 164, 174–175
Preserved Context Index System (PRE-CIS), 35, 64, 115, 150
Prévost, Marie Louise, 140, 142
Printed indexes, 37, 40, 170, 187
  arrangement, 46, 61
  compared with card form, 182
  free-language terms, 117–118
  search, 148
  source of terms, 178
  syndetic structure, 176
  use of thesauri designed for computer search, 31–32
  word frequency, 181
Production speed, derivative and assignment indexes, 110
Prynne, William, 8
Publishing, computer use, 11
Punched cards, 30–31, 42
Punctuation, 141, 146
  arrangement, 46, 49–52
  facet denotation, 159
  synthetic notations, 58–59

Q

Qualifiers of terms, 69–70

R

Raghavan, K. W., 141, 146
Ranganathan, S. R., 10, 158, 160
Rapid Selector, 11
Rare terms, 161–162
Recall and precision, see also Relevance judgments and prediction
  derivative and assignment indexes, 114–116
  effects on
    addition of access points, 118
    cross references, 72
    roles and links, 34–35, 151
  inverse relationship, 97
  KWOC and controlled vocabularies, 114
  limitations of studies, 6
References, see Cross references; Locators; Syndetic structure
Related terms, see Permissive cross references
Relative location, 9–10
Relevance judgments and prediction, 21–22, 26–27, 37, see also Recall and precision
Reports, indexing, 88, 92
Retrospective search, 26, 177–178
Richmond, Phyllis A., 64, 146
Roles and links, 34–35, 151–152
Rolling, Loll, 72
Ryan, Vincent J., 20–21

S

Salton, Gerard, 73, 123, 127
Saracevic, Tefko, 26
Sayers, W. C. Berwick, 57–58
Scattering of information, 72–73, 112
  derivative indexing, 106
  compared with assignment indexing, 110
  effect of syndetic structure, 183
Schlagwort indexing, see Keyword indexing
Schuegraf, Ernst, 181–182
Scope notes, 69–70, 73–75, see also Syndetic structure